A PARENTS' GUIDE TO
the Middle School Years

JOE BRUZZESE, MA

CELESTIAL ARTS
Berkeley | Toronto

Celestial Arts
an imprint of Ten Speed Press
PO Box 7123
Berkeley, California 94707
www.tenspeed.com

Distributed in Australia by Simon and Schuster Australia, in Canada by Ten
Speed Press Canada, in New Zealand by Southern Publishers Group, in South
Africa by Real Books, and in the United Kingdom and Europe by Publishers
Group UK.

Cover and text design by Toni Tajima

Library of Congress Cataloging-in-Publication Data
Bruzzese, Joe.
   A parents' guide to the middle school years / Joe Bruzzese.
      p. cm.
   Includes index.
   Summary: "A handbook for parents navigating the challenges and oppor-
tunities that arise when their children attend middle school"—Provided by
publisher.
   ISBN 978-1-58761-341-8
   1. Middle school education—Parent participation—United States—
Handbooks, manuals, etc. 2. Parent-teacher relationships—United States—
Handbooks, manuals, etc. 3. Home and school—United States—Handbooks,
manuals, etc. I. Title.
   LB1623.B78 2009
   373.23'6—dc22

                         2008055113

Printed in the United States of America
First printing, 2009

1 2 3 4 5 6 7 8 9 10 — 13 12 11 10 09

CONTENTS

ACKNOWLEDGMENTS

This book brings together more than twenty years of amazing moments with countless families who shaped my life through their kindness and generosity.

Moving forward wouldn't feel right without acknowledging a handful of people who stun me with their brilliance. Thank you to my wife, Kimberly. Your determination and sheer willpower to achieve leave me as breathless as your beauty. To my two children, Jordyn and Tristan, I couldn't imagine a world without you. Your courage inspires me. You are my heroes.

Thanks, Mom and Dad. Without your encouragement and confidence, I would not be the father I am today.

To my brother Dom, seeing you grow from a feisty young kid into a loving father moves me beyond words.

I owe special thanks to my sister Stephanie. Your gift for crafting diamonds from lumps of coal brought my dream to life.

I also want to acknowledge Jason Womack. Through a stroke of good fortune or perhaps fate, you changed my perception about what life could be, and for that I am eternally grateful.

Thank you, Paul Lee, for teaching me one of life's greatest lessons. Happiness can be found in a fortune cookie or a pot of boiling water.

Thanks to Larry Chambers for demystifying the publishing process.

Finally, to my team at Celestial Arts/Ten Speed Press, thank you for believing in me. A special thanks to my editor, Sara Golski. You possess the rare ability to inspire passionate writing while gently prodding a writer forward.

INTRODUCTION

Of the eight million children attending middle schools this coming year, the experience of only one of them—your own child—will truly change your life. Guiding your child's transition into adolescence takes time, patience, and a significant step forward in personal parenting knowledge. Mention the term *middle school* among a group of high school parents and you can see the sly smile sweep across their faces, a subtle sign that seems to suggest their happiness at having made it through *those* days. "What is it that they know?" you wonder.

The road through the middle school years can be smooth at times. Your child's grin as she talks about her wonderful new friends will send your spirits flying high. Positive progress reports can bolster your belief that your child will thrive. Indeed, the rise of positive emotions from exciting new changes can keep you and your child sailing across a sea of tranquility. But beware: the journey through middle school can also take you through turbulent waters.

How will you handle the inevitable adolescent crisis that leaves your child feeling frustrated, sad, or depressed? Changing your perception of what constitutes a crisis is one of the many adjustments required for understanding your child's frequent emotional shifts. A crisis could mean something as simple as a missing shoe or as serious as chronic bullying and drug abuse. Balancing a child's growing need for independence with genuine concern for his physical or emotional safety can become a never-ending exercise in patience for the parent who is accustomed to routinely "saving the day." True, at times you will be called on to advocate for your child when her physical or emotional safety is at risk. But although bullying and drug abuse call for strong parent support and presence, the occasional spat between friends or a challenging homework assignment rarely do. Instead, you should view many of these situations as valuable opportunities for your child to figure things out on his own—and grow in the process. You will likely find this oscillation between being an adamant advocate and a silent partner is an acquired skill that requires new levels of parenting savvy and self-confidence.

The emotional instability that often characterizes a middle schooler's move into adolescence can be exaggerated by the stress of a full academic load and a long list of extracurricular responsibilities. Although you may instinctively want to bring quick resolution to a series of scheduling snafus, I encourage you to stand down and hand over the reins of responsibility to your child for the management of her everyday schedules and routines. Shifting your parenting role from ever-present manager to supportive coach allows your child to gradually accept greater responsibility while benefiting from your continued guidance.

Great coaches inspire, teach, and celebrate achievement. Yet coaching your child through the middle school years will likely be a dramatic change from your earlier role as a teacher and manager in which you assumed responsibility for all of the decisions that impacted your child's day. Remember, middle school marks the beginning of the transition into adolescence and the development of increased independence. As a coach, you will still provide ample opportunities for your child to practice the skills you have taught him. But unlike in your previous roles as teacher and manager, you won't be called on to monitor your child's moment to moment progress. This news may come as a welcome relief to those parents who are ready to move forward toward a new and equally fulfilling relationship with their child. However, I also anticipate that a fair number of parents will struggle and resist letting go of their previous role and adopting what appears to be the more relaxed role of coach. If you are among them, I urge you in particular to take advantage of the insights, stories, and, in some places, step-by-step strategies I'll share that can ease your transition into the new and engaging role of coach.

Coaches need support too. Success is rarely achieved without encouragement and commitment from a team of valued individuals. You and your family may need to rely on the guidance and support of close friends to pull you through some of middle school's tougher moments. A team of people who care deeply about your child's success is a priceless resource to acquire. Teachers, coaches, mentors, and extended family members form a supportive team that will guide both you and your child through the gauntlet of challenges that lies ahead. If your recent attempts at sharing worldly wisdom with your child have already begun to go unheard, then the team-building ideas presented in the coming chapters may be of special interest to you. Taking on the responsibility for answering all your child's questions and providing solutions to all of life's challenges is an impossible task for parents alone to accomplish. You will strengthen your position as a parent by relying on a team of trusted individuals who know and support your child. Parenting today's middle schooler has truly become a team sport, filled with enough action to keep everyone engaged.

The need to rely on an extended leadership team throughout middle school is in keeping with the significant change in the traditional definition of *family*. Today, single-parent homes and families with dual wage earners nearly outnumber the traditional mom-stays-home-and-dad-goes-to-work households that many of the parents reading this book (and even more of *their* parents) knew as children. Families today can rarely find time to sit down and share a conversation, let alone a meal. The range of meetings, practices, and work-related commitments leaves many families hard-pressed to share one meal a week together. It may seem extreme to actually schedule a time to talk, but with the busy schedules many families navigate each week, time well spent together can be fleeting unless it is planned and thus becomes firmly rooted as a family priority.

I've written this book to inspire hope in the relationship parents and children share as they move through the middle school years. As I'll describe next, three themes run through the chapters: *building confidence, maintaining a connection,* and *overcoming challenges.* Families who thrive during the middle school years actively pursue each of these themes. Although the journey through middle school will not be free of frustration for any family, with an understanding of the three themes, your family is certain to grow in a positive way.

The following summaries offer a glimpse of the highlights from each chapter.

Chapter 1: In a sea of new faces, middle schoolers face the challenge of creating new friendships while maintaining friendships from elementary school. Chapter 1 looks at the issues surrounding the day-to-day life of peer relationships, including how to approach new people, handle bullies and cliques, and keep in touch with buddies from before. Jockeying for a spot in the collage of social groups can leave some kids feeling like they're standing on the outside looking in while their peers climb the social ladder. Although friends won't help your child over every bump in the road, a positive peer group certainly adds a boost of confidence for conquering the emotional peaks and valleys of the middle school years.

Chapter 2: Establishing a strong team of teachers (that may also include coaches, counselors, and other mentors) sets the stage for a rewarding academic experience. Chapter 2 provides a guide to building a solid team, helping parents learn the best times and ways to approach teachers and how to decipher teacher expectations. You will gain four tips for productive parent-teacher relationships and identify four steps to getting a smooth start to the new school year.

Chapter 3: Although some children benefit from the rigor of advanced or honors classes, the vast majority of kids fail to thrive if the level of challenge overwhelms their current academic ability. It can be hard to find the ideal setting that provides just the right amount of challenge. What's the answer? Chapter 3 presents a plan for how kids can thrive in the face of challenge, without becoming overwhelmed—starting by studying smarter, not harder. From five steps to buying the right supplies, to four ways for finishing homework in half the time, this chapter will guide you in the fine art of finding the right balance in your child's academic undertakings.

Chapter 4: Your child's extracurricular commitments can lead to late nights and mounting anxiety about how to excel academically while managing it all. Chapter 4 shows you how to help your child bring balance and organization to her extracurricular life. Learning how to guide your child toward a challenging, yet realistic set of goals remains one of parenting's most daunting tasks. With the plethora of opportunities available both before and after the school day, children and parents can quickly become sucked into an overloaded schedule. You can ensure a smooth start to the school year by identifying and committing to a few interests outside of the school day—settings in which kids can experience success in having met their academic responsibilities while simultaneously engaging in activities they truly enjoy. You and your child shouldn't require advanced time management skills to find time for both. With a proactive attitude—based on the creation of a vision for the coming year—your child will be well on the way to enjoying the best that both environments have to offer.

Chapter 5: Today's kids confront a host of new challenges that most parents have little experience with. As the information age evolves at an ever-faster pace, parents struggle to stay in the know about technology's latest trends. The average middle school parent needs terms like *social networking* and *cyberbullying* explained. In contrast, most of today's U.S. middle schoolers emerged from the womb into a wired world. Like the telephone, the Internet has become a mainstream form of communication for today's youth. Chapter 5 lays out a safe path through the Internet by identifying common myths about social networking sites like MySpace and Facebook, while providing tips for helping kids steer clear of trouble—like the hazards of sharing personal information with strangers and viewing inappropriate material.

Chapter 6: Finding the time to actively engage in family events keeps kids and parents moving forward in a positive direction. It will take a commitment from everyone in the home to create a vision for your family's continued growth. In the absence of a vision, families may become distant, more like individuals moving in separate directions than a tight-knit group held together by a common set of goals and interests. Each of the preceding chapters alludes to the importance of thinking beyond the moment; the final chapter focuses on uniting the members of your family through a commitment to ongoing communication in the coming years.

Building confidence, maintaining a connection, and overcoming challenge form a complete plan of action for thriving during the middle school years. Having worked with thousands of families as both a teacher and coach, I see each of these themes as critical to whether a family holds together or parents and kids move in separate directions. Your child's task—meeting the challenge of a seven-period schedule while trying to combat a case of unrelenting pimples—may seem small in scale compared to the challenges we face as parents. However, from your child's perspective, the onset of puberty and a bottomless pile of homework can quickly become cause for alarm and periods of self-doubt, followed by a dip in self-esteem. Developing a connection with the other adults who now will affect your child's life requires faith and confidence in your ability to move from your former role of teacher and manager to the role of supportive coach. Yet this journey—stepping back while allowing your child to step up to the challenge of becoming an independent person—is one that all parents hope to take. My hope is that you look back on the middle school years and smile, confident in the knowledge that your child has learned how to thrive in the face of challenge.

CHAPTER 1

Making Friends and Facing Foes

MIDDLE SCHOOL kicks relationships between kids up to a whole new level of ambiguity. In addition to the obvious shifts that middle school presents—like a new campus, a full complement of teachers, and an increased academic load—there are more subtle changes in a child's physical and emotional development that add complexity to the equation. The onset of puberty—in addition to the increased sense of self-awareness brought on by intense peer scrutiny—leaves many adolescents feeling emotionally insecure. Combined with the stress of an increasingly demanding academic load, these factors can make for some drama-filled friendships. If you had a hard time understanding the rhyme or reason behind these relationships before, it will likely seem even tougher as the kids become bona-fide teenagers.

"My daughter had her friend Julie over to spend the night last weekend. They were like peas in a pod, talking about movies, the kids at school, and the latest fads. Monday after school, I asked if Julie was planning to come over again. My daughter responded, 'I'll never speak to her again.'"

—*Lisa, middle school parent, Milwaukee, WI*

The jump from a reasonably solid set of friendships in elementary school to a somewhat shaky collection of acquaintances in middle school can be challenging for kids and frustrating for parents. It's hard to be patient as you watch your child careening back and forth between peer groups, trying to find the best fit. Just keep this in mind: adolescence is a time when a child experiments with different personas as she moves closer to identifying her true self-image. Exploring new social groups is a natural part of this process.

Before you decide that your middle schooler is definitely more challenged by friendships than the other kids, review the following three situations common among adolescent friends (as well as a few tips for how you can respond to them).

Best friends, mortal enemies

It's not at all uncommon for friendships and social groups to change from day to day in middle school, often without warning or explanation. Again, with adolescence comes a child's need to discover his real identity, and he often approaches this by trying out different social groups until he finds one that gives him a sense of belonging. The nuts and bolts of middle school can make this task particularly daunting, with the sudden shake-up of groups formed during elementary school and the greater number of students on the middle school campus compared with elementary school.

★ COACHING TIP

As new peer groups frequently form and dissolve, your child will almost certainly find himself left out at one time or another. Stand by for emotional support, but again, allow these normal adolescent ups and downs to play themselves out, and resist the urge to jump in and save the day. Your child may meet even your well-intended suggestions with a less than grateful reply. Avoid bruising your own relationship with your child—steer clear of the day-to-day adolescent drama.

Phone call fiascos

What starts out as a five-minute phone call between friends can quickly mushroom into a dramatic conversation that lasts the whole evening. These calls typically involve girls more than boys, as girls sometimes react with stronger emotion to the new gossip that's often spilled in a phone call, whereas boys may be quicker to dismiss the same information and instead wait for an in-person confrontation. There is one big exception: the phone call between boyfriend and girlfriend that ends in a breakup; in this situation, both sexes go through a series of emotional responses ranging from anger and frustration to sadness and depression.

★ COACHING TIP

If you suspect a phone call is going badly, after the call ends wait for a minimum of ten minutes (sometimes longer; watch for behavior that indicates an opening) before checking in with your child. A simple statement like "Let me know if you want to talk" is sometimes all that is needed to bring your child to a place where he can talk calmly about what happened on the phone. Avoid barging into the bedroom or picking up the phone during a heated call; this is likely to bring a wave of adolescent wrath crashing down on you. Space and time can relieve tension, so allow your child one or both when his emotions run to the extreme.

Appearance changes

In an effort to fit in, adolescents often change their physical appearance to look like other members of a particular group. Adolescents experience an increased urgency to find and be accepted by a peer group. From an adolescent's perspective, belonging to *any* peer group is better than being alone. These groups come together for different reasons, such as a similar interest in a sport, an extracurricular activity, or music. Once the group forms, it's common to see them wearing the same fashion styles and haircuts as a way to further express the group's shared identity.

Occasionally children enter middle school with one or two close friends who subsequently connect with a new group—leaving a few lost souls clamoring for friendship. Without a defined peer group of their own, these children may come together and create a unique identity. Rather than blending into the social background, these new social groups often make extreme changes in how they look (hair, clothes, piercings, and tattoos) in an effort to attract attention.

Friendships definitely play a crucial role in your middle schooler's ongoing emotional development. Best friends can become arch enemies within the span of a day, before again returning to BFF (best friends forever) status. This cyclical pattern inevitably leaves your child vulnerable to having her feelings hurt. Stand by, offer a supportive shoulder to cry on, but restrain yourself from trying to help solve your child's every friendship dispute. Your life can quickly become a soap opera of adolescent angst if you choose to take on the role of problem solver or peer mediator. No parent welcomes the sight of a teary-eyed child, but flying in to save the day doesn't give your child the opportunity to negotiate a relationship truce. Navigating the path between emotional confidant and supportive parent can be tricky, particularly when you're called on to welcome a new group of friends whom you know nothing about. You can both support your child and give her the freedom to find a peer group for herself by respectfully observing her circle of friends, without hovering too close or assuming the role of friendship manager.

You're probably thinking, *Good idea, but how do I pull it off?* One key is figuring out how to stay informed about your middle schooler without seeming intrusive or overbearing.

Smart sleuthing

When it comes to talking about the details of their friendships (and many other aspects of their lives), most middle schoolers develop and fine-tune their ability to use selective silence when parents ask questions. Parents try to engage the child in conversation and get one-word answers—or even no response at all. As their frustration grows, many parents settle for conversations that more closely resemble a game of Twenty Questions than a real conversation.

Why do kids seem to clam up at this point in their lives? The answer lies in their growing need to develop a unique sense of self. It's natural for adolescents to want to stake a sole claim to some part of their lives. So they typically view a parent's questions and comments about their lives as intrusive. They'll commonly answer with a short "That's my business" or "Why are you so nosy?" and then retreat behind the bedroom door.

Revisiting the birds and bees

As if it weren't challenging enough having to stake a claim to a particular peer group, many middle schoolers experience the pangs of romance for the first time. We called them crushes, and kids still use the term to describe feelings that range from "I would like to be more than friends" to infatuation. Crushes typically precede a move toward a full-fledged boyfriend or girlfriend relationship, but the awkward nature of expressing one's romantic intentions often brings any potential for a relationship to a halt before it can evolve into anything more lasting than a crush. Occasionally you may overhear your child use the phrase *hooking up* in reference to a recent sexual rendezvous between two classmates. When crushes move beyond the virtual connections of cell phone calls and online messaging to a sexual encounter, then the romance has moved to the hookup phase. Exploring intimate relationships rarely leads to physical contact beyond the occasional kiss, but the media's recent attempts to sensationalize sex during the middle school years may have you believing otherwise.

Although viewing any of the prominent daytime talk shows could leave you worried about the prevalence of sexual behavior among today's middle schoolers, the statistics tell a different story.

Recent research from United States Department of Health and Human Services does confirm the existence of sexual activity during the middle school years, but at nowhere near the epidemic levels that media outlets would have you believe. Although research indicates that some middle schoolers do engage in sexual intercourse and oral sex, the numbers are low in comparison to those in high school. This knowledge won't relieve the anxiety that comes from imagining yourself suddenly a middle-aged grandparent, but it does give you a wonderful opportunity to sit down and revisit the birds and bees conversation with your child.

The parents I speak to rarely express delight in talking with their children about sex, yet they are willing to put their own discomfort aside when considering the potential alternative—teenage pregnancy. Beginning a discussion about the consequences of becoming sexually active can be difficult, bordering on impossible, for the reluctant parent. Ease into the conversation by planning for some alone time with your child. A trip to the park, movie theater, or other public venue gives you an opportunity to share some meaningful time together. Refrain from having *the* conversation while driving in a car. The lack of face-to-face contact may be easier for you, but your child won't get to see your reaction to her questions, comments, and concerns, any of which might cause you to suddenly veer off course, causing a massive pile-up. Save yourself from potential injury; find a quiet place where you can give the conversation your complete attention.

It's hard enough starting a conversation about everyday issues; talking about a topic that's implicitly uncomfortable ups the ante. But your discomfort is an indicator of just how important this topic is. So be honest and jump in with both feet. Even an opener like "I want to talk about relationships" or "Is there anything you want to ask me about sex?" doesn't really get to the heart of what you really want to talk about. Opt instead for a straightforward statement that shares both your intent and concern; something like, "I know kids your age are having sex, and I want to make sure you have answers to questions you might be wondering about."

Yes, it's blunt and initially shocking for your child to hear you say the word sex, but it brings the elephant in the room from a dark corner to center stage, where you can begin to have a conversation about a topic that every child wonders about at some point on the road to adolescence. Whether or not your child has thought of or is currently engaging in sexual behavior, he or she will have questions. Without a parent's guidance, kids will often seek answers from other trusted adults. In the absence of their qualified advice, your child will turn to her peer group. Heading down a path in the dark while being led by a person who's blindfolded doesn't sound like a safe way to travel. Turn on the light for your child, so she can see the path ahead and feel confident about the choices she will make in the coming years.

Times to talk

Here are some suggestions for opening up the lines of communication. Kids anticipate the inevitable blast of parent questions at the end of a school day or over dinner. Choose instead to wait and listen. Instead of dominating each attempt at conversation with your own questions, try to say less and let your child do more of the talking. For example, let silence fill the space during car rides home from school (or, if your child takes the bus or carpool, during the initial after-school moments when the two of you meet up at home) instead of immediately asking questions. You may have a couple of quiet rides or moments, but eventually your child will likely share a comment about the day. As the words begin to flow, wait until you have the opportunity to add a comment or ask a question that will prompt further conversation. A lot of kids actually like to talk if given the opportunity. What they don't appreciate are a rapid-fire barrage of questions and the continued probing of what they perceive to be nosy parents. In time, your less-is-more approach will be rewarded by a more talkative teen.

A child's one-word responses to your questions can bring a conversation to a halt at the outset. Try asking questions that begin with "How" rather than "Why" or "What." Such questions hand ownership of the conversation to your child. When you ask "How did you do that?" or "How did you find out about that?" you set the stage for your child to take control of the conversation. Remember, your purpose is to keep the conversation moving. Asking questions with yes-or-no answers will bring most discussions to a halt; questions that begin with "How" can keep an adolescent talking for hours. "How did you do so well on your test?" or "How did it feel when you heard the news?" are two examples of questions that acknowledge a child's ability and emotions, and acknowledgment stimulates conversation. By contrast, questions beginning with "Why" put kids on the defensive. "Why did you do that?" or "Why didn't you try it the way we talked about earlier?" require the child to justify his actions. The adolescent mind perceives a "Why?" question as an accusation of wrongdoing. The natural reaction to this accusation can turn a lighthearted conversation into a series of short negative exchanges. Staying focused on your child's enthusiasm and interests can keep "why" questions from creeping in and smothering your together time.

"Aidan hardly ever talked until the day I realized I wasn't giving him a chance to. I stopped peppering him with so many questions all the time, and he started opening up. Now he jumps into the car after practice and immediately starts talking about the players and coaches. He goes almost nonstop for our entire thirty-minute trip home."
—John, middle school parent, Phoenix, AZ

Beyond the everyday conversations you should strive to achieve with your child, you may also have opportunities to gain valuable information about his day through casual observation. And when it comes to observation, rule number one is to keep your distance. Observing is different from hovering: although observing casually from a distance will provide you with information about your child's social circle, hovering over your child by following him onto and around the school campus will almost certainly embarrass both your child and you.

Look for and plan times when your presence will not be noticed by your child. The minutes following the morning drop-off or immediately preceding the afternoon pick-up can be wonderful observation times: when kids come together at school, their focus shifts to each other, which leaves you with a few moments to observe from the safe distance of your car, getting a glimpse of your child's body language and overall demeanor while interacting with his friends as he walks into school or toward the car. Sports practices and games can be another venue for similarly unobtrusive information gathering. On the flip side, showing up at school or at an event unexpectedly in an attempt to gain a front seat to your child's social proceedings can end badly. You may even do this unwittingly when you suddenly find yourself cast into a crowd of your child's peers at a party pickup or after-school event. The less-than-subtle look on your child's face will be a clear indicator that you don't belong—and the cold shoulder that follows will reinforce this. When these inevitable moments occur, try a simple apology to your child. A statement like "I will try to stay farther away next time" may not gain you immediate verbal acceptance or forgiveness, but your child will know you're aware of how important the social part of his life has become.

A middle schooler's social life doesn't end at the conclusion of the school day. The prolific use of cell phones and text messaging can keep kids connected late into the evening hours. To bring more conversation back into your relationship, try identifying times and places where your child is not allowed to use the cell phone. Make your home a no-cell zone; this doesn't mean no phone calls, rather, all social calls must happen on the landline phone. This doesn't make it OK to listen in on your child's phone calls, but it does give you the chance to keep an ear tuned to the first few minutes of the conversation—just long enough to find out who's calling and why. If you're genuinely concerned about what you hear, after she has hung up, try simply saying, "Let me know if there's anything you want to talk about." This may be enough to get your child to open up about the call.

Practice these tips by planning for short exchanges or casual observations throughout the week. Look for moments when you might share a few minutes of conversation over dinner or in the after-school hours before bedtime. If the weekdays seem crammed, look ahead to the weekend for a time when you might take a short drive or share lunch while taking on a few errands. It may seem hard to carve out time in a busy schedule, but the extra effort can earn you the invaluable reward of a deeper, more open relationship with your child, in which she is more likely to take your good advice on ways she can succeed in middle school—including how to make new friends.

Though most new middle schoolers will naturally tend to look for familiar faces from elementary school, the hundreds of new kids on a middle school campus represent a great opportunity to add new friends to the mix. Give your child a leg up by reassuring her that you remember how challenging it can be to meet new friends in middle school—and offer the following three tips to make it easier:

1. **Just say "hi."** Starting a conversation with a complete stranger is challenging for most middle schoolers (and for some adults, too). Sometimes the easiest way to begin is by saying "Hi." Typically, students begin arriving at school fifteen to thirty minutes before the opening bell. In the early days of the school year, your child will naturally be looking for a familiar face; encourage your child to say "Hi," or just smile in the direction of a few new people along the way. She'll have another chance to share a smile, a quick "Hi," or a "What's up?" while walking through the halls between classes. Having made a few friendly gestures during the morning hours, your child is primed for the lunch break—where short conversations can develop into budding friendships.

"My best advice to new students is to smile and say 'Hi' to everyone they see here on the school campus."

—Veronica Rogers, junior high principal, Goleta, CA

2. **Find a group.** The lunch area is teeming with potential friends. Encourage your child to look for a table full of kids that includes a familiar face from one of his morning classes and join them. In shared conversation over lunch, kids often identify common interests. With these connections, kids begin to form new circles of friends.

3. **Get involved.** Before the school year begins, many schools send out information about all of the extracurricular activities that will be available in the coming year. Taking part in these activities is one of the best ways to meet new friends, so be sure to talk about the options with your child and decide on a few to try (we'll talk more about how to make these extracurricular choices in chapter 4). With a slate of activities in place, your child will be able to ask other kids about the activities they plan to join—giving him one more way to build a new group of buddies.

Out with the old, in with the new

Meeting new friends doesn't mean old friends are forgotten. Maintaining friendships from the elementary school years helps children smooth out their transition into middle school. The sense of familiarity created by seeing well-known faces around campus and in the classroom can soothe the anxiety of being surrounded by new faces. Staying connected with old friends often opens us to meeting new people who may become part of our social circle.

Most of us have difficulty remembering where we first met the people who are now among our circle of close friends. Spouses aside, we generally can trace the first conversation of a budding friendship only to a range of time (say, sometime during the middle school years) rather than a specific moment (say, November 1, 1989, at the mall, while sharing a root beer float). Our difficulty in recalling the beginning of friendships is due in part to the many impromptu conversations we have with new arrivals (friends of friends) to our current circle of friends. We meet these friends of friends through a series of continued interactions that eventually lead to identifying common interests. Middle school offers a bevy of similar opportunities for expanding a child's social circle. Encourage your child to maintain old friendships; they hold the possibility of meeting new friends.

The process of meeting new friends isn't always a happy one. As kids sort through their new mix of schoolmates, power struggles may arise. As new social circles form, dominant personalities emerge, and many children experience for the first time the phenomena of bullies and cliques. You can help minimize the unpleasantness of schoolyard ruffians and queen bees seeking social status by equipping your child with a set of proactive skills.

Cliques: a fact of middle school life

Unpleasant as they may be, cliques are an inevitable part of the middle school social environment. Cliques are a lot like the middle school social groups described earlier, with one important difference: they often refuse to accept new kids into the group, even those who share similar interests. These members-only social groups comes to the forefront in middle school as children become interested in more socially oriented activities. During elementary school children are encouraged to stay active on the playground before school and during break periods. On a middle school campus, the larger student population and lack of space discourage this level of physical activity. Changing the social dynamics of student interactions would require an overhaul of the supervision system and a new look at where students could spend their break periods. Currently, students mill around common areas on campus, which are patrolled by school administrators and faculty. At many middle schools the ratio of students to administrators or faculty heavily favors students, leaving opportunity for potentially dangerous behavior. For now, it's safe to say that the school setting for adolescents is fairly uniform and predictable, which unfortunately means that cliques are here to stay.

"Being popular is the only place to be. If you're not in the popular group, people think you're a loser."
> —*Angela, seventh grader, Nashville, TN*

Why do kids continually attempt to fit in with groups that want to exclude them? Usually, they see the status and security that comes with group membership as worth the potential rejection or abuse. To the new middle schooler, the prospect of walking the halls alone and being seen as a loser seems far worse than any possible abuse from being on the fringes of a popular group.

The new middle schooler should start learning early on to avoid the heartache of clique exclusion and instead to develop healthy peer relationships. For a child eager to connect with a new group of friends, it can be difficult to differentiate between potential friends and foes. You may need to coach your child in how to steer clear of bullying situations and cliques. It's crucial that kids learn how to identify cliques, particularly those groups of children who like to exclude or bully based on appearance, interest, or race. Although the short-term benefits of belonging to a clique may seem inviting to the child who is looking for higher social status, the ultimate consequences are often exclusion and hurt feelings. Encourage your child to stick with friends who offer positive support, and remind her that it may take time to find the right niche.

Bullying in all its shapes and sizes

Although clique encounters can initially lead to hurt feelings, these often become easier to ignore once your child finds her own group of good friends. Bullying, however, takes exclusion beyond hurt feelings to serious abuse. The classic stereotype of the bully is an older, more physically imposing boy threatening and beating up a smaller boy. Yet today's forms of abuse extend beyond this style of aggression. Although physical abuse still occurs among adolescents, the incidence of emotional bullying through electronic means—cyberbullying—is on the rise among both boys and girls, thanks to the anonymity of the Internet and cell phones. These virtual media have given bullies new avenues to inflict fear without having to cause physical harm. For example, a seemingly innocent picture from the weekend slumber party can be easily distorted and sent on to hundreds of people.

Whether bullying happens in person or online, parents need to step up and advocate for their child. The following six warning signs can serve as clear indicators of bullying behavior. Separately, each sign could raise concern. Observing more than one of these behaviors in your child is definite cause for action.

Reluctance to leave home. If your normally social child chooses to stay home rather than go out with friends, it may be because of a bully. Bullying can occur at school as well as at off-campus social events. In the crowded corridors typical of many middle school campuses, bullies often lurk where traffic is heaviest—leaving their victims little room to escape. With limited school personnel to monitor student movement between classes, passing periods can become a game of cat and mouse for some students. The school cafeteria presents another challenge for students. Lunch lines are easy targets for bullies in search of a few extra dollars. Leaving school might seem to offer relief from bullies, but abuse that begins on campus usually continues off campus. Social environments such as parties or the movie theater have great potential for bullying incidents. Without the supervision of an adult chaperone, kids are free to interact in any way they like, often to the detriment of a few unfortunate souls.

Missing activities. If your child declines to attend sports practices, games, and other extracurricular activities, this may be a sign that your child is being bullied. The attention of coaches and supervisors is occasionally diverted away from the team or group to talk with referees and parents for a moment or two. In those moments, kids can quickly find ways of singling out an individual, engaging in verbal taunting and subtle physical abuse (pushing and tripping) that can go undetected.

"Drive me, please!" A child who pleads with you to drive him to school rather than taking his normal bus route may be trying to avoid confrontations on the bus. With a load of twenty-plus middle schoolers on the bus, bullying can easily go unseen.

Unexplained cuts or bruises. If your child can't offer a reasonable explanation for the appearance of any unusual marks on her body, it's time to investigate.

"In the rush to get the kids moving in the morning, we don't have a lot of time to spend together. I mistook my son's anxiety about getting ready for school in the morning for an attempt to prevent us from getting out the door. I later found out he had been bullied for over a month. I didn't see it."   —Dana, middle school parent, Denver, CO

Increased sadness or anxiety. Adolescents tend to be moody; however, a sudden increase in crying outbursts and anxiety levels could be your child's reaction to being bullied.

Steadily decreasing academic performance. A dip from 95 percent on one test to 85 percent on the next doesn't warrant a full-scale investigation. But repeated low scores, missed assignments, or comments from your child's teachers about declining performance are signals that may mean there are bullying issues at play.

Even if you suspect your child is being bullied, the question of what to do about it can be difficult—especially if your child hesitates to communicate with you. Here are three things you can do to unearth a problem without requiring a flood of details directly from your child:

1. **Share observations.** Offering statements like "You seem sad today" or "This seems like a rough week for you" may open the door to a conversation with your child.

2. **Investigate.** During all the hours your child spends at school, your contact with her is generally limited to, at most, a few quick phone calls. You can fill in the gaps of what you may be missing by sharing a conversation with the adults who actually see your child in the school setting every weekday. Teachers, coaches, and mentors can be an invaluable source of information about a child's life. If you are concerned about your child's behavior, turn to this group of adults for insight.

3. **Make contact.** A casual argument between friends doesn't call for a visit to the school, but when arguments turn physical or include verbally abusive statements, don't hesitate to schedule an appointment with the school counselor. Bring the evidence you have from your observations as well as any conversations with adults who regularly interact with your child.

Bring bullying to an end

It may take time to end bullying at your child's middle school. While you investigate and share your concerns with the school's administrators, your child will need a plan for confronting bullies should the challenge arise. Sharing these three methods with your child at the start of the school year will help to prevent potential bullying later.

---

1. **Speak up.** Bullies will continue to abuse and harass their victims until someone says, "That's enough!" Unless bullies are told to stop, they believe what they are doing is acceptable. Although speaking up against bullying behavior may be enough to stop it in some cases, be aware that this approach may not work in all situations (in which case your child can try methods 2 and 3).

2. **Travel with a group.** When kids travel as a group, bullies lose their courage, because a group means more people who might stand up and take action.

3. **Ask for help.** Talking to a friend or an adult about a bully can help to put a stop to the abuse. Teachers are more aware of bullies now than they have been in the past, so reinforce the idea that approaching a teacher for help is OK. If your child is shy, she could also express herself by writing a short note to the teacher, naming the bully and what she doesn't like about the way she's being treated.

"I was afraid to get on the bus, go to class, and walk down the halls. Text messages and voice mails kept coming. The worst part was I didn't know who the bully was. I didn't want to tell anyone because I thought it would get worse. I finally decided I didn't want to live like that anymore. I went to a teacher and asked for help. My life got

*better after that. The bullying stopped and I felt safe going to school
again."*   —*Sam, sixth grader, San Francisco, CA*

Cyberbullying: the online bully

Cyberbullying—using electronics like cell phones and computers
to harass and intimidate—has become the preferred method for
many bullies in middle school (and even in high school). Hiding
behind the cover of a friend's cell phone or an anonymous internet connection, bullies can threaten their victims with less fear
of getting caught.

★ COACHING TIP

In most bullying cases, kids don't want to tell an adult for fear that the
abuse will increase when the bully is identified. Like victims in most abuse
situations, bullied kids may also feel responsible for somehow encouraging
a bully's abusive behavior.

So how do you help your child deal with a cyberbully? During
your next family meeting or weekly check-in (see chapter 6 for
more information), bring the topic of internet safety to the table.
You may be surprised by the wealth of information and suggestions your child has when it comes to staying safe online. Before
sharing your own thoughts, ask your child for a few of his. Among
the ideas you list on your family's plan for online safety, consider
the following. MySpace and Facebook have become common additions to many middle schoolers' social lives. If your child uses
websites like MySpace or Facebook, consider keeping his profile
of personal information private. Chapter 5 takes a detailed look at
both services and specific actions you can take to limit the sharing of personal information. Email is becoming less common
among teen and tweens, but if your child still uses it, a shared
family email address can dramatically reduce the possibility of
bullying messages reaching your child. Sharing access to this

account allows parents to monitor for any potentially threatening messages.

As email becomes less popular with today's generation of kids, their use of cell phones seems to increase. Cell phone use and abuse can be more difficult to monitor than the family email account; however, limiting incoming and outgoing calls to a pre-selected set of phone numbers can effectively reduce the chance of bullying while simultaneously keeping the monthly bill to a minimum. Your cell phone provider can help you filter and block numbers from your child's phone. Calls and text messages are likely to form the bulk of bullying threats. The now common addition of a camera on most phones has created a new medium for bullying behavior. An innocent shot snapped quickly between classes can eventually find its way into a bully's hands, becoming a weapon for teasing. Encourage your child to stay clear of impromptu camera shots; this will help minimize this threat.

As with all other bullying incidents, the moment you become aware of a threatening email or phone call, or see anything online referencing your child in a negative way, report it to school administrators. Contacting the school is the first step to pulling the plug on cyberbullying.

Cell phones: middle school dos and don'ts

Check the backpack of just about any middle schooler, and you're bound to find a cell phone. These phones have become a fact of life for almost everyone from middle schoolers on up to adults. Middle school students should know that having a cell phone is a big responsibility, and they need to use it wisely.

Your child can avoid the unpleasantness of having a teacher confiscate his cell phone if, before the school year starts, you take the time to review with him a few basic expectations. In general, schoolrooms and cell phones don't mix. The school cell phone policy should be spelled out in the student handbook. Reading this policy with your child can prevent his phone being confiscated later.

Many teachers have their own rules about students bringing phones into their classroom. Review each class syllabus for specific cell phone rules. Teachers may have a separate set of expectations governing cell phone use in the classroom. The first time a phone accidentally rings, most teachers will issue a warning. The second time, your child may not be so lucky. Repeated "accidental" ringing usually results in the loss of a phone—or worse. Some teachers have even been known to give detention to students who won't keep their ringers off during class. Stashing a phone out of sight, preferably in a backpack, is the best way to keep it from being taken by a teacher (or anyone else). The same rules apply to talking and texting. Teachers have become wise to the evolution of text messaging. Using a phone to text friends during class risks the same undesirable consequences as making a phone call.

★ COACHING TIP

Talk with your child about responsible cell phone use *before* the school year begins. Agree to a set of expectations that you both can live with. Talking about the consequences before a problem arises can save you hours of frustration and needless arguments.

Speaking of texting, most middle schoolers now spend more time sending text messages on their cell phones than making actual phone calls. If your family doesn't have a monthly cell phone plan with unlimited messaging, the first monthly bill after your child enters middle school can give you a shock. Avoid this unwelcome surprise by reviewing your family's monthly call plan. Most cell phone plans come with a limited number of text messages as part of the monthly fee. Sending more messages than what's included in your plan incurs extra fees that can add up quickly. If you suspect your child's flurry of messages will send the monthly bill skyrocketing, take a few minutes to review your expectations for the cell phone's use, as well as the consequences for acting irresponsibly. Sketch out a plan that seems reasonable for both you and your child. You may require that your child contribute the added expense for unlimited messaging or pay for any overage minutes, particularly in cases of repeated overuse.

Drugs and alcohol, by the numbers

As addicting as text messaging can appear to be, the long-term effects of an overactive cell phone pale in comparison to the far more serious and certainly more addictive behavior that drugs and alcohol can create. Among the challenges that kids and parents face in the middle school years, exposure to drugs and alcohol ranks at the top of the list. Although some children will have their first experience with either one during elementary school, middle school can mark the beginning of a behavior pattern leading toward addiction. With greater numbers of students on campus and a mix of older adolescents with younger ones, the opportunity for experimentation and exploration increases.

Although it may be hard for parents to imagine a twelve-year-old child drinking or using drugs on a weekly basis, the latest statistics tell a different story. Consider the following five facts (statistics provided by the Marin Institute, www.marininstitute.org):

1. Every day, on average, 11,318 American youth (ages twelve to twenty) try alcohol for the first time; 6,488 try marijuana, 2,786 try cocaine, and 386 try heroin.

2. Alcohol is by far the most used and abused drug among America's teenagers. According to a national survey, nearly one third (31.5 percent) of all high school students reported hazardous drinking (more than five drinks in one setting) during the thirty days preceding the survey.

3. Children who are drinking alcohol by seventh grade are more likely to report academic problems, substance use, and delinquent behavior in both middle school and high school. By young adulthood, early alcohol use is associated with employment problems, other substance abuse, and criminal and other violent behavior.

4. Young people who begin drinking before age fifteen are four times more likely to develop alcoholism than those who begin drinking at twenty-one.

5. Alcohol is a leading cause of death among youth, particularly teenagers. It contributes substantially to adolescent motor vehicle crashes, other traumatic injuries, suicide, date rape, and family and school problems.

Despite the seriousness of these statistics, don't panic—by reading this book, you're already taking steps toward ensuring that your child avoids drinking and drugs. Implementing the following three actions will support your child in pursuing a drug-free life.

Supervise after-school activities. Parents can minimize the potential for alcohol and drug abuse through close supervision of after-school and weekend activities. A quick phone call to a friend's parents can often confirm the supervision of another trusted adult and prevent an encounter with drugs or alcohol. However, it requires a certain degree of trust to rely on the integrity of fellow parents to remain present and responsible for your child's welfare. Sharing a cup of coffee with parents who are new to your child's social circle can raise your trust level and lower your anxiety about after-school gatherings. You can make sure your child's activities, whether at home or in public, are supervised, without becoming overly intrusive. Your presence nearby, although not necessarily in the same room, is enough to give most adolescents a sense of accountability. If your concern or curiosity reaches its limit, don't hesitate to ask about after-school outings. Most kids won't be very forthcoming with the details of their social gatherings, but it doesn't hurt to express your interest by asking, "How's it going?" or "What are you up to?"

Show you care. Regularly letting your child know "I'm here if you need me" without bombarding him with constant questioning both shows him you care and encourages him to open up on his own.

"I struggled to maintain a relationship with my son Alex during his middle school years. His resolve to gain independence was unrelenting. He'd say things like, 'You can trust me, Mom,' so I gave him almost unlimited freedom. Later, I'd find out he'd been at a friend's house, unsupervised for hours and into all kinds of trouble."
—Caitlin, high school parent, Jasper, WY

Establish expectations. Before the school year begins, share your expectations for after-school and weekend activity participation. Are weekends open for an unlimited number of outings with friends? Or does your vision for the year include family time every week? What's your policy on your child hanging out with friends after school? Is it OK for your child to have friends over without supervision? What about a trip to the mall or the movies—will these types of group activities require a chaperone? Having a clear set of expectations in place will alleviate the need for continued debates throughout the year.

What kids need to know about drugs and alcohol

Most elementary schools now educate kids about the effects of alcohol and drugs in the primary grades (kindergarten through third grades). Drug awareness education typically continues each year, gradually increasing in depth and complexity. Children across all grade levels generally observe Red Ribbon Week, an annual effort in the campaign to expand drug and alcohol awareness.

Build on this foundation by talking with your child about the four serious side effects of alcohol and drug use below before the school year begins. Discussing substance use and abuse with your child sends a clear message: *I care about you and recognize there may be tough times ahead.* During this same discussion, it's important to talk about the difference between *use* and *abuse.* Without this distinction, a parent's occasional glass of wine with dinner could be perceived as alcohol abuse. Tackling these challenging issues during the adolescent years strengthens the connection between parent and child—the strong bond you both may need to get you through some of life's most challenging moments.

★ COACHING TIP

Before sharing your personal thoughts about how use and abuse differ, ask your child to share her thoughts; you may find that she's already fairly clear on the difference. You may need only to clarify small misunderstandings.

There are four serious side effects of drinking and drugs:

1. **Impaired physical and mental function.** A brain affected by alcohol or drugs has difficulty making wise decisions and sending signals to the right muscles needed for talking, walking, and most seriously, driving.

2. **Overwhelming fatigue.** Alcohol and drugs sap the body's energy, making you feel exhausted.

3. **Emotional changes.** The parts of the brain that control emotion are affected as well, making you feel anger, sadness, and depression.

4. **Life-threatening side effects.** Vomiting, difficulty breathing, and death can result from consuming large amounts of alcohol or drugs in a short period of time.

Dealing with depression

As if all the aforementioned topics weren't enough for your middle schooler to deal with, stress-driven depression can also set in around this time, as he tries to cope with the many social, emotional, and physical changes he's experiencing. Transitional times can trigger increased anxiety in today's middle schoolers. The uncertainty of a new school year, coupled with the potential for academic overload, is enough to frazzle an adolescent mind. The end of long breaks like the winter holiday and spring break have potential for trouble as well: returning to the routine of early morning wake-ups and full nights of homework can make your child feel overwhelmed—a precursor of stress-driven depression. You'll be able to tell the difference between the occasional mood swing and truly stressful times by watching out for the following five warning signs:

1. **The fun is gone.** When hanging out with friends or going to practice isn't fun anymore, your child is probably stressed about something.

2. **Missing school.** Occasionally staying home from school because of illness is OK, but missing a lot of school mainly because your child just doesn't feel like getting out of bed may be a sign of too much stress.

3. **Lack of energy.** Feeling tired at the end of the day or as she rolls out of bed in the morning is normal. Falling asleep in the middle of the day could mean her body is feeling the effects of stress.

"Andrew had a bit of a meltdown after a recent game, but I'm actually surprised it didn't happen sooner. It was due to a combination of school expectations, soccer, and other activities. We worked through his breakdown by focusing on the right now—that minute—and then moving on. Later, when he'd had a chance to calm down, we figured out a plan for how he'd achieve his objectives over the next three to four days. He was extremely relieved."

—*Carol, middle school mom, San Antonio, TX*

4. **Changes in eating habits.** Eating more often than normal or constantly feeling hungry are two common signs of stress. Eating a lot less than normal or completely losing the appetite are also signs of stress.

5. **Changes in sleep patterns.** Middle schoolers need approximately nine hours of sleep a night. Sleeping for twelve or more hours may be a response to a series of stress-filled days.

When adolescents experience these changes, the last thing they may want to do is to be around other people—especially parents. However, because prolonged stress often leads to depression, you'll want to alleviate the stress through proactive strategies. Here are ten tips for how you can help your child reduce stress in his life:

1. **Have regularly scheduled family dinners.** At dinner time, ask everyone to talk about what happened during the day—including at least one good thing. This can be small ("I didn't have to wait for the bus—it came right away") or major ("I got a B on my science test").

2. **Be health-minded.** Encourage the whole family to take care of the three basics—eating well, sleeping enough, and exercising regularly.

3. **Make laughter a priority.** Watch funny TV shows and movies together. When you hear a joke that you like, remember it to share at home.

4. **Let go of negative feelings.** When conflicts or bad moods seem to get out of hand, call for a time-out. Any argument can benefit from a walk around the block to cool off.

5. **Create quiet times.** No TV, no music, no computer—just make an environment conducive to meditation, reflection, reading, or rest. You may need to negotiate this with a child who's used to practically round-the-clock sound.

"About midway through the school year my son's English teacher asked the class, 'How do you know when you're too busy?' I cringed when I heard my son's reply, 'When I can't remember the last time I saw my friends.' I had forgotten about what mattered the most in his life."
—*Dawn, middle school mom, San Diego, CA*

6. **Pitch in.** As a family, help one another. For example, if your child is struggling to complete a school project, other family members can collate reports, staple exhibits on a display board, or bring in a snack.

7. **Celebrate.** Mark not just birthdays, but accomplishments like a child's improved report card. No gifts are required; simply saying "Congratulations," initiating a round of applause, or writing a note of acknowledgment will get the point across.

8. **Welcome friends.** Encourage your child to invite friends over and have them stay for dinner or a sleepover.

9. **Inspire.** Talk with your child about goals, making plans, and thinking ahead. Show that you take your child's goals seriously and will do what you can to help.

10. **Create an action plan.** Planning can help your child handle a worrisome challenge. Divide the task up into parts she can manage. A one-step-at-a-time approach divides and conquers anxiety.

Taking the time to familiarize yourself with the social issues your child will face in middle school is half the battle. You now have a stronger grasp of those issues and are more prepared to support your child throughout the ups and downs of her middle school journey. Supporting your child through the roller coaster ride of middle school wouldn't be possible without help from a team of qualified kid experts. One of the greatest benefits of the move to middle school is gaining not one, but a minimum of four new teachers. Your child's composition of teachers forms the core of your parental support team. The relationship you establish with this group of individuals will significantly impact your child's growth for years to come. Building a relationship requires work from both ends—teachers and parents. In the coming chapter, we'll discuss how to establish strong and supportive relationships with all of your child's new teachers.

CHAPTER 2

Building Solid Relationships with Teachers

FOR BOTH STUDENTS AND PARENTS, forming good relationships with teachers is another important piece of the middle school pie. This process can prove challenging for parents. For one thing, you'll find that middle school teachers try to raise the level of student accountability by first confronting students directly with questions or concerns about achievement before bringing issues to a parent. This can be disconcerting at first; after all, during your child's elementary school years you've grown accustomed to being the first to receive word about your child's progress or lack thereof. But by approaching the student first, teachers compel the student to play a more active part in his school experience. Of course, this presents a new challenge to your child as well.

You can support your child during this developmental shift by working to build your own strong relationships with his middle school teachers. Together you, your child, and your child's teachers can form a network of mutual support that leads to a successful middle school experience for all of you.

Teachers: middle school versus elementary school

Before we talk about how to form good relationships with your child's middle school teachers, consider the following perspectives from parents whose children have already been through middle school:

"Middle school teachers are often perceived as more heavy-handed, while elementary teachers are seen as more nurturing."
—Sarah, middle school mom, Dayton, OH

"We were pleasantly surprised by the warmth and enthusiasm of our son's [middle school] teachers. The fall orientation days gave us a chance to meet and talk to his teachers and the school administrators. Somehow, meeting everyone in person set our minds at ease."
—John and Lisa, middle school parents, Denver, CO

"I noticed a broader range of personalities. It took my kids by surprise when they entered middle school. Some teachers, even elementary teachers, are project-oriented, not people-oriented."
— Ann, mom of two middle school boys, Ojai, CA

"With seven classes on her schedule, my daughter was in for a real challenge. In addition to the increased work load I was really surprised by how different each teacher was when it came to assignments, tests, and project requirements."
—Jackie, middle school mom, San Diego, CA

For many kids, middle school marks the first time they will travel from classroom to classroom to learn from a variety of teachers who each cover a specific subject, rather than remaining in the same classroom with a single teacher for an entire day of study. Clearly middle school teachers are a varied group of individuals, yet they share a common set of requirements when it comes to what they expect from students during the first few weeks of the school year. The following tips can help your child get started on the right foot with any teacher.

1. **Arrive on time for each class.** Punctuality will play a big part in helping your child to build a positive first impression with his teachers—but he'll probably need some help in this area, as the single-classroom structure of elementary school has not given many new middle schoolers an accurate sense of how long it takes to travel between classes. From the moment the bell signaling the end of one class rings, your child will have several minutes to arrive on time to his next class. Encourage your child to consider saving longer conversations for the longer morning break or lunch period. Add a wristwatch to his list of back-to-school supplies; it's an invaluable tool for promoting prompt attendance, because late arrivals often translate into teacher-issued tardy marks. Although teachers may stretch the transition time by a minute or two during the first few weeks of class, if your child continues to slide in after the bell he will face unpleasant consequences. Trips to detention and study hall are often used to deter future late arrivals; however, what most middle schoolers don't always realize is how a teacher perceives a student who is chronically tardy. Being perceived as a student who lacks respect for a teacher's time can create a barrier between the teacher and student. A record of too many tardies can also adversely affect a student's overall grade. Be sure to review the school's tardy policy with your child to avoid any misunderstandings about the school's daily schedule.

★ **COACHING TIP**

Teachers like to review their expectations repeatedly during the opening weeks of school, emphasizing what's most important to them. For example, if your child hears a teacher tell the class over and over again about the importance of homework, she can expect a large portion of her final grade to come from homework assignments. If another teacher talks a lot about tests, this is a tip that studying well for tests is a good idea.

----

2. **Share ideas and ask questions.** Class participation also contributes to a good impression. Most teachers base a portion of a student's final grade on it. So even if everyone else is trying to keep a low profile, encourage your child to share some thoughts during the class discussion. Middle schoolers can be reluctant to stand out in ways that might attract their peers' attention and get them labeled a know-it-all. Try giving your child a friendly reminder about making a positive first impression; this can help him overcome his initial apprehension.

3. **Work ahead.** Completing assignments and projects before they're due results in both better grades and a less stressful school year for your child—and for you. To help your child develop this skill, find five minutes to sit together and scan each class syllabus for the words *late work policy.* If those words are followed by *No late work will be accepted*, make a mental note to put these classes at the top of the homework priority list. Also, keep in mind that although many teachers accept work after the deadline, they give lower grades to late assignments. The best strategy is to finish all work by the deadline if not before.

4. **Come prepared.** English class is usually a no-brainer when it comes to materials. If your child brings the class textbook or novel, notebook, and a pen, she'll be ready for anything. Math and science classes often require additional accessories (calculator, compass, protractor, lab books, and so on). Help your child compile a list of required materials for each class. Encourage your child to check the list between classes; this can help her avoid the stress of showing up to class unprepared.

Do any of these tips sound familiar? In many ways, middle school rules and expectations are similar to those in elementary school. The challenge for your child will be to adjust to the subtle rule changes that come with a roster of different teachers, each with a unique personality, preferences, and expectations. Coaching your child to look and listen for these differences early in the school year will help minimize misunderstandings later.

"Taking the time to review each syllabus with my son gave me an overview of the entire year. Knowing there was a plan in place set my mind at ease." —Nancy, middle school mom, Ventura, CA

Making sense of the syllabus

Fortunately, most teachers hand out a syllabus on the first day of school. Most syllabi include everything the teacher wants your child to know about the class (such as grading policies, homework policies, and an overview of the year). Understanding this road map will dramatically increase your child's chances of meeting the teacher's expectations. The idea of learning the rules may sound easy; the hard part is taking action on what you know.

It takes time to sift through six or more syllabi, so plan this activity for an evening when you will have at least thirty minutes of uninterrupted time with your child. Find a highlighter and ask your child to mark the answers to the following questions on each class syllabus:

1. **What's the homework policy?** When should assignments be completed? Is homework assigned every night or once a week? Are assignments handed in or kept in a notebook for review at a later date?

2. **How will final grades be determined?** What percentage of the course grade is based on homework versus projects, tests, participation, and attendance?

3. **What materials are required?** Does your child need to bring any materials (notebooks, binders, and so on) in addition to the class textbook?

4. **Can you contact the teacher outside of class if you have questions?** Look for a phone number, email address, or class website.

★ COACHING TIP

Teachers occasionally offer students extra credit opportunities. Middle schoolers have a tendency to live in the present, not considering the possibility that they might need a few extra points at the end of the quarter. Suggest to your child that she take advantage of every extra assignment or challenge that a teacher offers. Even though these assignments may seem unnecessary, extra points add up over time. Given that it's hard to predict what your child's grade will be at the end of the quarter, having a few extra points in the bank may come in handy. The other benefit to completing extra credit is that teachers come to understand more about your child and how she learns. The standardized format of assigning the same nightly homework for the whole class leaves little room for kids to show their unique learning abilities and interests. By taking on extra assignments or self-selected projects, a child offers teachers new insights into that child's life—insights that can strengthen the relationship between teacher and student and add further depth to the learning experience.

Talking with teachers

After your child goes through the class syllabus, he may still have lingering questions, best addressed by asking the teacher directly. Even if your child doesn't need to speak with his teachers right off the bat, chances are he will at some point during the year—and that means a one-on-one conversation.

★ COACHING TIP

Teachers often arrive early in the morning or remain in their classrooms during lunch or after school. Consider an early morning drop-off or late pickup one day during the week so your child may be able to check in with a few teachers outside of the traditional school day. For quick questions, it's OK to contact teachers by email or making a phone call. But when your child has a question about content information, an email or phone call may not be the best method.

If talking with teachers makes you or your child nervous, don't worry: we'll look at two approaches to initiating a conversation—one for teacher-child discussion, the other for teacher-parent interactions. Some children find it hard to talk one-on-one with their teachers. Traditionally, children are not given many opportunities to talk with adults, particularly those in positions of authority, so taking the initiative to address a teacher outside of the formal class discussion can be a challenge. Your child may find starting a conversation with his teacher especially daunting in the midst of a busy school schedule, with only a few minutes in between classes. However, middle school is when your child begins the journey toward independence and responsibility for his own progress at school. For this reason I encourage you to promote teacher-child conversations whenever possible.

So what's the best way for your child to catch a teacher to discuss a question or concern? Review the following four-point plan, then take ten minutes to role-play a conversation your child could have with a teacher. Take turns playing the roles of teacher and student so you can model how the conversation might flow from both perspectives.

I. **Prepare for progress.** Your child should think about the question(s) he wants to ask and what information he hopes to gain prior to asking a teacher for assistance outside of class. Coaching your child through the process of clearly articulating his concern can make the difference between a truly rewarding interaction and one that leaves him feeling frustrated. If your child's questions are related to something learned in class, then brainstorm a list of specific questions about the content. Encourage your child to steer clear of general statements like "I don't understand any of this," which don't pinpoint where help is needed.

If homework is the challenge, suggest that your child bring specific questions or problems to the meeting. A word of caution: questions about tests should be focused on learning the information that was missed rather than making a plea for a better grade—unless, of course, there is a concern that the test was graded incorrectly.

2. **Engage.** A few opportunities to role-play the conversation will prime your child for an engaging and rewarding meeting with the teacher. On the day of the meeting, simply ask your child, "How do you feel about talking with your teacher today?" This general question leaves the door open for any last-minute role-play or advice you can offer. Occasionally, kids will ask for a few last-minute pointers, but most are ready to tackle the challenge independently. At this point your role as a coach is complete. It's time for your child to step into the game and use the skills he has practiced.

3. **Ask for time.** Begin by asking the teacher the following question, either before class begins or right after the class is dismissed: "Is there a time today or tomorrow when I could talk with you about a question/concern I have?" Your child's goal is only to schedule a time for a conversation, so encourage your child to resist the temptation to start discussing the specific concern at that time, particularly if it's about the course content. The ideal time to talk with a teacher is during a break when the teacher can give your child five to ten minutes of uninterrupted time.

"My son was scared to death about the possibility of confronting his teacher with questions about what he didn't understand. He took the plunge and met the teacher anyway after some encouragement from his mom and me. Later I received an email from his teacher who told me how excited he was to see a student taking responsibility for his achievement. What an incredible step forward for our son."
— *Jim, middle school dad, Denver, CO*

4. **Follow-up.** Follow up with your child after the meeting: "How did things go with Mr. Smith today?" Your child's initial reaction will tell you more than his words might. A long sigh usually means that the meeting could have been better. A broad smile could mean that the meeting went exactly as planned. Try to refrain from a round of twenty questions. Remember, this was your child's chance at sharing a meaningful conversation with an adult authority figure. Feel content in the knowledge that you had a hand in coaching your child to the point of initiating a conversation. That said, it's perfectly acceptable to send the teacher an email or leave a short voicemail expressing your gratitude for the time he or she spent talking with your child. If there was anything notable in the conversation, you can bet the teacher will either call or respond to your email with the pertinent details.

Building a relationship with middle school teachers

It can be hard for you to start standing on the sidelines as your child begins to assume responsibility for talking with teachers. Throughout elementary school, it's usually the parents and teachers who communicate about a child's academic progress. Teacher conferences typically include only parents. In those years, you may also have welcomed the occasional impromptu conversation with a teacher when you dropped your child off at school or when you volunteered as a classroom helper. But when your child starts middle school, although you are still a valued partner in the education process, this changes; your role shifts from primary advocate for your child to more of a supporting role, as your child starts becoming his own advocate.

Understanding how and when to talk with teachers can open the door to supportive relationships—and sometimes, even new adult friendships—that will benefit both you and your child.

★ COACHING TIP

Most teachers see an average of 150 students pass through their classroom each day. Multiply 150 students by a teacher's tenure at the school and you have a person with considerable middle school experience. If you suspect that your child has a concern or question that he may be reluctant to share with a teacher, consider calling or emailing the teacher to gently suggest an impromptu conversation with your child at school. Teachers can be a wonderful source of wisdom for a child, particularly when that child is tuning out a parent's words.

One good way to identify the best times to talk with your child's teachers is to know a few of the *least* opportune times. For example, the two minutes before the class begins is one of the least available times for teachers and carries the added negative of extreme embarrassment for your child. It's also taboo to seek out teachers at school on the weekend, when they need a quiet break from the routine of the work week to catch up on classroom organizing, paperwork, and the like. This taboo extends to phone calls over the weekend and public places like the grocery store, shopping mall, and sports venues. Although teachers may be difficult to contact face-to-face during standard working hours, parents actually have a greater opportunity to connect with teachers and school personnel than in the past through—you guessed it—email and telephone calls.

Don't wait until Back to School Night to introduce yourself. Get off to a good start by following these four tips for productive parent-teacher relationships:

Make contact early. Sift through the pile of papers that your child brings home the first week of school. Look for contact information for each of your child's teachers. Create a contact list with any information you can find. With your contact list in hand, start making calls or sending emails. The ideal time for this is during the second or third week of school, as week one is hectic for everyone. Generally by week two classes are more in sync, and teachers will have time to respond to your messages. Finally, post the list in a visible location for future reference.

Focus on the positive. After reading through the class syllabi, choose something positive to comment on in your initial conversation or email with teachers. "The outline of class assignments in the syllabus is very helpful. Thank you for taking the time to lay out the scope of the year" is a powerful statement that tells a teacher you care about your child's learning and appreciate the time and effort the teacher has invested. Commenting on the inclusion of a teacher's biography or the promise of challenging course content also creates a positive impression about your commitment to the school year and your child's learning.

Connect in person. When Back to School Night finally arrives, make your way through the crowd of anxious parents vying for the teacher's attention and warmly introduce yourself. Your past efforts at communication will have paved the way for a solid relationship in the year ahead.

★ COACHING TIP

Keep your email or phone call brief. The goal is to introduce yourself with a quick, positive comment about the class and upcoming school year. A lengthy call or email can flag you as another overbearing parent who wants to take control of his or her child's year in middle school.

Maintain contact. Continue to build your relationship by sending an email or leaving voice mails every three to four weeks to share something positive (your child's enjoyment of the class, the interesting selection of readings, and so on). If you ever need to discuss a challenging topic such as academic progress or a peer-related issue, it's more likely your questions will find a welcoming ear.

Your initial connection with teachers is meant to lay the foundation for a year-long relationship. Given that children spend a significant number of their waking hours at school, teachers play an essential role in your child's life. With their support and encouragement, both you and your child will be better able to thrive in the months ahead.

When to get involved

Through short, ongoing conversations with their teachers, most kids will weather most issues that arise during the school year. However, some conflicts require additional attention and support from both teachers and parents. Relentless taunting from a school bully is one extreme example that warrants a conversation among teacher, child, and parent outside of school hours. Failing grades or a series of missed assignments (a precursor to failing grades) would also necessitate a more formal discussion involving everyone. It can be hard to define the line between what should and shouldn't prompt a parent-teacher-student conference. Use the following list of situations and suggested actions as a quick guide for differentiating between issues that warrant parent intervention and those better left to a child and teacher to sort out.

Situation: Your child spent the first week of school ranting about how strict his math teacher was, using the word *unfair* to describe his anticipated homework load. He pleads, "Can I switch to a different class?"

Suggested action: Do nothing, outside of acknowledging that school can be challenging at times. You can try sharing a personal story about a difficult teacher from your past, though that probably won't do much to diminish your child's angst. Don't assume the problem solver role; your budding middle schooler is capable of taking on this challenge. You can, however, monitor your child's progress by asking to see graded assignments and tests. If the academic rigor exceeds what you consider to be realistic, then send a brief email to the teacher inquiring about how you can support your child's ongoing achievement. If his progress remains stagnant or begins to head south of the C range, ask for a formal conference.

Situation: Midway through the academic quarter, you open the mailbox to find your child's progress report. Verbal assurances from your child over the past few weeks that everything was "fine" left you unprepared for the less than satisfactory tally of grades you now see.

Suggested action: Before picking up the phone or heading to the computer to set up a formal inquiry with your child's teachers, take a few minutes to talk with your child. Unless the grades border on failure, give your child a chance to brainstorm a list of ideas for academic improvement. If you jump in too soon with a barrage of helpful hints (or a warning of severe consequences), you strip your child of all responsibility for personal improvement. An informal sit-down with him is often all it takes to generate a list of new strategies. Lectures and severe consequences result in short-term changes at best. You have a better chance of seeing long-term positive change if, with your support, your child makes a firm commitment to act on his own ideas for improvement.

Situation: Your child's course schedule has been challenging from the beginning of the quarter. Nightly assignments and test preparation keep her studying late into the evening hours. The extra effort at home hasn't translated into improvement at school. Over the past three weeks, her test grades and assignment results have slipped significantly. When you've tried to offer her support, she's responded with irritation, assuring you "Everything is fine" and "Just let me deal with it."

Suggested action: Kids tend to achieve at a fairly consistent level over time. A rapid descent in academic achievement is a signal that something is amiss. A child's reluctance to discuss the issue is further cause for alarm. In this case, your first step should be to contact the school. Try sending a brief email or leaving a voice-mail, expressing concern for your child's recent academic decline and asking for suggestions about how you can offer additional support. If a teacher's response indicates an equal level of concern, then suggest a short (twenty minute) meeting during after-school hours in which both you and your child can talk with the teacher. Although most adolescents balk at the idea of a three-way meeting, their attendance is absolutely essential if any long-term changes are to be achieved.

Situation: Tension at home has reached an all-time high. With the exception of an occasional hello and goodbye, your child now communicates in short grunts. Although the recent report card shows solid marks, your usually jovial child seems caught somewhere between frustration and sadness. Repeated invitations to engage in family activities are met with little enthusiasm.

Suggested action: A few poor academic outings or a recent blowup between friends coupled with the emotional changes brought on by puberty is the classic recipe for adolescent angst. When asked, most adolescents can't articulate a single reason for their emotional swings. Don't hesitate to talk with adults who affect your child's life. Connect with teachers, coaches, and adult mentors; they can be an invaluable source of information and support. Often the other adults in your child's life have observed some of the same behaviors but dismissed them as isolated incidents. By gathering a variety of perspectives from the important adults in your child's life, you can gain a more complete picture of what may have led to your child's current emotional state. In a typical weekday he will spend more time with adults outside the home than with his parents, so it's in your best interest to keep in contact with this group of influential adults.

A well-established relationship with your child's teachers prepares both of you for the first of many formal achievement benchmarks: progress reports. The uncertainty associated with progress reports can be anxiety-producing, even for the high-achieving child. The self-imposed pressure to excel often keeps high achievers in a perpetual state of stress as they wait for confirmation of their progress.

Avoiding progress report shock

About four weeks after school starts, your child's first progress report will arrive in the mail. Of course, you hope the report will be cause for celebration. Inevitably, though, some students (and parents) suffer from progress report shock when they see their grades, because they hadn't paid attention to exactly how well (or poorly) they were doing. To avoid this anxiety, try a slight shift in thinking: instead of dreading the report, consider looking forward to it as an opportunity to affirm achievement and take action on any challenges it may present. One way to begin this shift is to encourage your child to be proactive about monitoring her progress by asking the teacher for an informal progress report every two to three weeks. The following two-minute check-in strategy is a short, structured approach that your child can use for initiating a conversation with any middle school teacher.

After the first several weeks of school have passed, suggest that your child stop by each of her classes either before or after school with the goal of spending two minutes talking with each teacher about her progress. Here are some sample questions to use during this conversation.

★ **COACHING TIP**

For adolescents to truly benefit from informal progress reports, they must obtain them without continued prodding from their parents. As soon as a parent starts to demand rather than suggest an informal report, the child no longer owns the reporting or achievement process. Overly eager parents can diminish their child's interest in school and achievement by trying to take over the learning process, essentially sabotaging their child's progress toward independence. Rather than assuming responsibility for your child's success or failures in school, anticipate the sense of fulfillment that comes from watching your child achieve, independently of your effort and influence.

"Hi, Ms./Mrs./Mr._____, I just wanted to stop by and ask you about how I'm doing in your class. Is now a good time, or should I come back?"

Once the teacher invites your child to continue the conversation, she can ask,

"Am I missing any assignments or projects?"

"How can I improve my grade in your class?"

"How can I challenge myself this quarter?" (An especially good question to ask if the child already has an A!)

The insight your child gains from these informal progress reports can be an invaluable part of her growth during the school year. Adolescents naturally yearn for independence. Taking responsibility for talking with teachers, particularly about academic achievement, gives adolescents a real opportunity to become more independent. Teachers begin to anticipate these informal conversations and provide more detailed feedback for your child. The ongoing communication with teachers helps your child develop greater confidence in her ability to talk with adults in authority positions, which feeds her ever-growing desire for independence.

From a teacher's perspective, your child's initiating these conversations translates into a genuine interest in learning. Teachers love to work with students who show a passion for learning. Beyond the strictly academic information children receive, informal progress reports provide additional opportunities to build relationships with the valued members of their support team—a skill that will serve them for years to come.

★ **COACHING TIP**

The hours outside of school can be busy for teachers, so encourage your child to be persistent in efforts to find a time for a two-minute check-in with each teacher.

Put the tools we've talked about in this chapter to work, and you will be rewarded with strong teacher relationships that ultimately lead to a much easier trip through the middle school years. Much of academic progress is based on the relationships children have with their teachers. Everyone remembers a few teachers who didn't rank very high on the likeability scale. It's hard for a student to make progress in a subject if he has a strained relationship with the teacher. By contrast, the school years you spent with some of your favorite teachers were undoubtedly filled with highlights and marked by significant progress. Considering the academic rigor most kids find in their middle school curriculum, it helps to have a team of teachers who are personally invested in their progress.

Of course, relationships alone won't make up for missing assignments or not preparing for the weekly math test. At some point your child must step up and take responsibility for putting in the effort necessary to learn and achieve. For kids new to the middle school routine, confronting a full backpack of homework can be overwhelming. Chapter 3 is focused on connecting you and your child with tested and proven strategies for getting things done in the after-school hours. We will look specifically at ways to sort through and organize what needs to be done, so when your child does sit down to begin the evening study routine she feels confident she can complete a list of assignments without taking the entire evening to do it. Let's look at the ways in which you can help your child complete homework efficiently and effectively.

CHAPTER 3

Getting Ahead in Class and Staying There

BUILDING STRONG TIES with teachers and connecting with a positive peer group set the stage for your child's successful middle school experience. After the school day ends, kids face the reality of a full night of studying. Some middle schoolers report spending upward of five hours a night completing assignments and studying for tests. Creating a plan for tackling the rigors of a middle school day begins weeks ahead of ever setting foot on the school campus.

Mind mapping the road ahead

In the weeks leading up to school, find thirty minutes of uninterrupted time to share with your child in *mind mapping.* The goal of this activity is to create a vivid picture of your child's year-long goals. Ask your child to choose a location for the mind mapping activity. A trip to the park or a favorite restaurant for lunch may set the stage for a productive brainstorming session.

A road map is most useful when you can identify two things: where you are and where you are going. Knowing what you have already accomplished is a valuable step toward achieving a goal. Most teachers, parents, and students focus on where they're going, often beginning with the end in mind. However, there is great value in first thinking about where you are now, and *then* setting your sights on where you would like to be—the goal.

Choose the medium (talking, writing, or drawing) that best fits your child's personality, then guide him through the following steps:

Step One: Ask your child to think about his experiences as an elementary school student. Brainstorm ideas in the following areas: learning strengths, weaknesses, challenges, interests, and dreams. When your child begins to run out of ideas, ask if it would be OK for you to share any additional ideas.

If the brainstorming format doesn't produce any ideas, consider free-writing for five minutes, in response to the following questions. If talking seems easier than writing, consider recording your child's ideas on a voice recorder.

1. What do I really enjoy about school? What do I like to learn about?

2. What has been easy for me to learn or do in school? What challenges me?

3. Where would I like to see the greatest change in my academic success?

4. If I could study *anything* at all, and learn about it, what would it be?

The ideas from your conversation, free-writing, or brainstorm will become the road map for defining your child's year-long goals.

Step Two: Take all of the ideas from step one and suggest that your child choose one of the following activities: write a letter, create a collage, or draw a picture that includes her ideas. Encourage your middle schooler to post her mind map in a visible location as a continued reminder and source of motivation for achieving dreams and meeting challenges. As new ideas and achievements emerge, your child can add them to the map.

Step Three: At the end of each academic quarter, take thirty minutes to review the map with your child. Add any recent accomplishments as well as new challenges for the coming quarter. A mind map has incredible power to focus a child's activity and achievement during the year, much as an atlas has the ability to guide us on a direct course toward our destination.

Step Four: At the end of the school year, take a few moments with your child to reflect on the many challenges, goals, and achievements that added up to a successful middle school experience.

★ COACHING TIP

Follow your child's lead during this activity. If you sense he would rather write than talk, give him an opportunity to jot down his thoughts on paper. Even kids with a preference for talking about ideas need a chance to record their thoughts in writing or in pictures, so remain open to a variety of different strategies for collecting and recording the information.

Creating a plan for the future will help your child plot a smooth path to achieving her goals in the coming year. But plans alone won't be enough to complete the journey. Move from planning into the action portion of the middle school year with an efficient and economical trip to the school supplies store.

Economical shopping

The annual shopping spree for school supplies signals the official return to school for kids and their parents. The average family spends upward of $500 a year on school supplies. Over 50 percent of school spending is thrown away on items that look necessary, yet often find their way into a drawer or trash can within weeks of the start of school.

The key to economical shopping is creating a list of what you need before the spending begins. Office supply stores are ready and waiting for the unprepared parent. You, however, will confidently stride past the suggested list of supplies at the storefront and begin the search for the necessary items on your list.

Creating a list

To avoid any uncomfortable arguments during the shopping trip, before you set out, take ten minutes to sit with your child as she assembles her list of supplies, using the following instructions as a guide.

Step One: Fold a piece of paper in half and label one side "Supplies for School" and the other side "Supplies for Home."

Step Two: List the following items under the "Supplies for School" heading:

- One box of pencils (twenty-four pencils)
- One box of pens (twelve to twenty-four pens)
- Highlighters (four to six)
- Three wireless notebooks with perforated paper (eighty to one hundred pages with three holes prepunched in the paper). These notebooks are different from the spiral-bound notebooks. Wireless notebooks have paper you can tear off along a clean edge.
- Backpack (Look for a backpack with two to three pockets. Keeping your books and binders separate from your supplies makes it easier to find what you need when you need it.)

You can anticipate that most teachers will hand out a class syllabus listing any additional supplies students will need during the first week of school. Buy a binder and any remaining supplies only after confirming they are needed. Binders add extra weight to a child's backpack that may not be necessary.

Some of your child's teachers may require a separate binder for their classes. For classes with a lot of written assignments, look for the heavy-duty version or a zippered organizer. Binders take a fair amount of abuse during the year, and cheaper binders fall apart, usually at the most inconvenient times.

With the list of school supplies complete, focus your attention on materials that will be used at home. An important part of succeeding in school is creating a study space at home that has everything your child needs for completing homework assignments and projects efficiently. Homework takes long enough to complete when all of the necessary supplies are present. The key to saving time and minimizing frustration at home is stocking the study space with a complete list of supplies before the school year begins.

Step Three: List the following items under the "Supplies for Home" heading:

- Two packs of loose-leaf paper (aka binder paper, usually found in packs of 100 or more)
- One box of pencils (twenty-four pencils)
- One box of pens (twelve to twenty-four pens)
- Two packs of 2 x 1$\frac{1}{2}$ sticky notes
- One stapler, desktop size (The mini-size version holds only about five staples.)
- One box of staples
- One box of large paper clips
- One three-hole punch (Buy the heavy version—it will last for years to come.)
- One file crate (The traditional egg crate variety will do the job.)
- One box of hanging files (which fit neatly into the egg crate)
- One desktop calendar (Check the range of months and get one that begins in the summer months and continues through the following year.)

- One pack of index cards (3 x 5 or 4 x 6)
- One pencil sharpener (handheld or electric)

Suggest that your child post the supplies list next to her study space and check the stock of supplies on a monthly basis; this helps to minimize the need for emergency trips to the store the night before a project is due. As items begin to run low, your child should be the one to suggest a trip to the store for restocking. Middle schoolers are ready to begin taking responsibility for their own supplies. Take advantage of this opportunity to begin slowly transferring responsibility for ongoing management of school to your child.

With both lists complete, you are ready to head to the store. At the store, shift the responsibility of locating all of the supplies to your child while you lounge in the comfort of an overpriced desk chair.

A word of caution: Before proceeding to the checkout line, take a thorough accounting of the items in your shopping cart. Be prepared for the addition of accessory items that were not a part of the original list. You can approach this challenge in a variety of ways.

Negotiation: *"Before we leave the house I tell my daughter that if she wants anything that is not on the list then she needs to pay for those items out of her own money."*   —*Pam, middle school mom, Tucson, AZ*

Needs versus wants: *"My standard response is, 'If you don't need it, I'm not buying it.'"*   —*John, father of two teenage boys, New York, NY*

I'll pay half: *"We negotiate the purchase of things she wants to have versus what she needs to have. I agree to pay for half of what she wants."*   —*Lisa, eighth grade mom, Dallas, TX*

Each of these strategies comes with its own set of challenges. The "Negotiation" method leaves the door open for a shopping cart full of accessories that might add more clutter—and therefore less organization—to a child's year. The positive side of negotiating purchases is that your child may begin to appreciate the cost associated with school supplies. This increased awareness could translate into a higher level of care and personal responsibility for the items you have purchased. Using the "Needs versus Wants" strategy may be best if your child has already become accustomed to budget-based shopping. Before embarking on your shopping safari, consider creating a budget of expected expenses with your child's help. This team-based approach to building a budget adds a layer of challenge and excitement to your trip. Will you be able to stay under the estimated budget? Or will the allure of scented markers put your final bill over the top? Working together may alleviate the desire to add unnecessary items to your bill. The only downside to eliminating additional items comes when trying to implement this strategy with a child who enjoys the extras. If your typical shopping experiences include the occasional discretionary item or two, then consider the third strategy—"I'll pay half." A mom of two shared this strategy with me years ago after I asked for some sage advice about parenting adolescents. For me, what started as a strategy for school supply trips has become a standard for most of the nonessential items my children want. Paying half of the bill encourages kids to think about which purchases really warrant spending additional time working around the house to earn the needed money. One note of caution: this strategy can prove challenging for the parent whose child earns a significant allowance. Expenses may begin to creep up when these same kids see the opportunity for frequent shopping trips on which Mom pays half.

Whether you decide to opt for the proactive process of negotiation or the "I'll Pay Half" arrangement, arrive at the store with a commitment to one of these strategies. Arguments over nonessential items can leave you and your child feeling embarrassed amidst the crowd of other shoppers. Locating and purchasing the right supplies is the first step toward becoming more organized.

A little extra effort to organize the supplies before the school year begins will pay off later when teachers begin to heap on assignments and projects. While other kids are spending time looking for materials, your child will be completing assignments. That organized study space you've created together can lead to more efficient, effective study sessions.

Creating study central

Building a house requires a specific set of tools and materials; tackling the academic challenge of a middle school day takes a specific set of tools and materials as well. Designating a specific location for all school-related activities is the first step in a series of tasks designed to bring organization to your child's year.

Kids can (and do) study in a variety of locations. The traditional desktop setting may not be the best location for your child to get things done. The kitchen table, family room, or the back seat of your car are other likely candidates. When scouting out the ideal space with your child, consider the following as optimum conditions for completing homework activities:

1. Is there adequate lighting?

2. Are electrical outlets within reach?

3. Does the space have a hard flat surface?

4. Are there any distractions?

5. Is there space to house supplies?

If your child appreciates the structure that a desk can provide, you're in luck. All of the supplies you purchased can live happily within a few desk drawers. But a growing percentage of middle schoolers have become mobile, opting to change study venues on a regular basis. Changing locations can eat up valuable minutes unless each study location has a full set of supplies. Creating multiple sets of supplies can be a costly alternative. Consider, instead, the mobile supplies station. Large lidded plastic containers can house all of a student's supplies for easy transport around the house or in the car if need be. An alternative to carrying large tubs around the home is a moveable cart.

The goal of any study space is to provide a comfortable environment with quick access to supplies. With comfort and accessibility, the task of getting things done becomes more efficient.

Milk crates: America's premier filing system

With six or more teachers to contend with, it's only natural to assume that there will be a substantial increase in the volume of paper that travels home with your child. Plan to cope with this influx of paper by setting up a filing system before the school year begins. The milk crate has evolved from its humble roots as a multipurpose carrying case to an economical filing solution. You can find office versions of the milk crate stacked high on the shelves of most office supply stores, waiting to be filled with a set of hanging files. At a retail price of just under $5, there isn't any reason to opt for a highly stylized $20 version. With your child, retrieve the plastic tabs that came with your set of hanging files. Label each folder with the name of one class.

★ COACHING TIP

Attempting to organize your child without her direct participation will ultimately result in frustration (both yours and hers).

Using the filing system

Learning to use any organizational system takes some time and energy. The good news is that the time and energy are relatively minimal in comparison to sifting through a semester's worth of paper in your child's backpack. The key to maintaining any filing system is creating a regular schedule for moving papers into the file folders. The typical middle schooler can hold out for a month before moving papers from his backpack and binder into the file crate. Every two weeks may be a more realistic interval, depending on the flow (or flood) of paper your child brings home. At the end of each grading period, take some time to reevaluate how the filing system is working.

The volume of paper can change during the course of a year. Teachers are famous for sending home a stockpile of assignments at the end of a grading period. If you can predict when these deluges will occur, mark the date on the calendar and plan for a filing party. Regardless of when that occurs, try to establish a consistent time and schedule for emptying the binder and backpack into the file crate. As with any new routine, the first few attempts take more effort to complete than will be required after the routine becomes a habit. Kids need the most support from parents during the early stages of building a new routine. Here are some tips for supporting your child through the organizational process.

1. **Plot a date.** After coming to a mutually agreed upon interval for filing papers, record the first date on your family's calendar. This date recorded on the calendar dramatically increases the chance that your child will follow through.

2. **Discuss consequences.** Equally important is your child's understanding of the consequences (both positive and negative) associated with completing this task. If your child chooses to follow through with his plan to file all papers, then a celebration is order (see number four). However, if the date comes and goes without the papers being filed, then it's your role to follow through with the agreed-upon consequences. Stick to your guns here. The power behind setting an expectation quickly disappears if it turns out to be nothing more than an empty threat.

3. **Ask, don't tell.** Filing is an organization strategy that your child can learn. For this strategy to become a part of your child's toolkit, he needs to take responsibility for using it. You don't have to keep prodding or cajoling. When the day arrives, ask this question: "When are you planning to file your papers? I noticed that today is the day we marked on the calendar."

4. **Celebrate success.** When your child completes the first official filing of his papers, celebrate. Celebrating can be as simple as sharing an acknowledging statement: "Hey, you did a phenomenal job filing your papers. I appreciate you taking responsibility for keeping your schoolwork organized." The second part of this acknowledgment reinforces a bigger issue—responsibility. Although the file crate may look neat, learning to assume responsibility for staying organized is the real reason to celebrate. The power of acknowledgment, particularly with middle schoolers, cannot be overstated.

Building a binder

In association with a backpack, your child's binder is the critical link between school and home for all assignments and parent–school communication. It can be a challenge to create a system that meshes with your child's preferences while meeting his teachers' demands. The binder setup we describe here is meant to provide your child with a starting point for building an organized binder. As teachers become more explicit in their expectations, your child can adapt the binder to meet the new demands.

Prior to engaging in this activity with your child, confirm that you have the recommended list of supplies that follows. Running to the store midway through the setup will put a halt to your momentum.

- One heavy-duty or zippered binder
- A package of six to eight binder dividers with folder sleeves

- One seventy-page wireless notebook
- Heavy-duty three-hole punch

To set up the binder, label each binder divider with the name of one class. Insert the dividers in the same order as the class schedule. The first class of the day belongs to the first divider in the binder and so on. Insert a wireless notebook after the last divider. Each divider has a pocket on the front side. This is a temporary home for any papers that are not three-hole punched. Encourage your child to make a choice about where new additions to the binder will go; then refrain from offering additional advice.

Ask to see the binder after the setup is complete. If your child can articulate how his system works, then consider the task complete. Check in regularly (every two to three weeks) to confirm that the system he started with is still working. If papers appear to be falling out or you hear complaints about lost assignments, take the opportunity to sit down with your child and brainstorm ways to overcome the challenge.

Like the file crate system, the setup steps for a binder are easy to complete. The challenge with both systems is maintenance. Creating a regular routine for filing papers and hole-punching the remaining papers will ease the stress of trying to stay organized. Papers tend to pile up quickly in a binder, so consider a schedule that will keep the binder looking good on a weekly basis. Removing or hole-punching papers can usually be done once a week; however, there are always exceptions. The English teacher who loves to read, write, and copy everything he reads and writes can lead his students to a binder explosion in a few days.

An efficient study space, together with a filing system and an organized binder, minimizes stress during study time while maximizing the time spent working on homework activities in the after-school hours. With the foundation for your child's home organization system in place, let's turn our attention to a new and equally challenging space to organize—the school locker.

Locker organization

The task of setting up and maintaining a school locker presents a wonderful opportunity for children to practice taking responsibility for the ongoing upkeep of a space outside of the home. Parents should consider their child's school locker off limits unless an emergency warrants access. The responsibility of maintaining a locker rests solely on the shoulders of the child. Given the small dimensions of most middle school lockers, the possibility of losing supplies remains relatively low, and thus the chance for organizational success is high. However, without a plan for organizing the space, your child's locker can easily become an extension of her bedroom or backpack—with assorted goodies sticking out of every available nook and cranny.

With the goal of creating an organized space, consider purchasing the following supplies for your child:

- One to two locker shelves with supports (found at most office supply stores)
- Six magnets
- Two sticky note pads
- Small box for extra pens and pencils
- Magnetic container large enough for pens, pencils, and sticky notes

The challenge for middle schoolers is to gain entry to their lockers, stash unneeded items, and gather supplies for the coming class, within the span of four to five minutes. This wouldn't be nearly as challenging if it weren't for the hundreds of other kids who are scrambling to do exactly the same thing at the same time. Encourage your child to adopt a trial-and-error mind-set when it comes to her locker setup. As with most new organizational systems, lockers require an adjustment period that includes time to remove and reposition supplies. After a few minor changes, kids generally find a setup that enables them to reach each class on time with all the required materials in hand.

If your child asks for help or complains about having difficulty reaching class on time, then offer a few ideas. Proceed cautiously. Being asked for your assistance does not give you license to assume ownership and responsibility for maintaining your child's locker. Instead, suggest a few minor changes, like stacking textbooks and notebooks together by class or taking supplies for two or three classes during a single visit to the locker. Kids particularly like this suggestion because shuttling supplies back and forth after every class takes time that could be better spent socializing with friends.

Remember, transferring responsibility to your child is a process that takes time. If you offer too many potential solutions for confronting locker woes (or other common dilemmas), you'll slow down the transition to independence.

Here are several locker dos and don'ts to discuss before school begins:

- Do return or replace materials in their original location.
- Don't throw materials into the first available space in your locker.
- Do use magnets to hold up important papers and keep other papers in a binder.
- Don't leave papers lying around inside your locker.
- Do give yourself at least one month to learn a new system.
- Don't expect your locker to organize itself.
- Do take responsibility for your materials. Now is a great time to take on more responsibility and become more independent.
- Don't expect anyone else to organize your locker or backpack.

I'm here; now where do I go?

Middle schoolers in the first few weeks of a new school year often have trouble remembering their locker location and combination. And returning after every class to retrieve a new set of materials can also add extra stress to an already busy schedule of events. You can help alleviate your child's anxiety—and raise her confidence that she *can* successfully navigate the halls and arrive safely at each destination—by helping her create a map of the school campus.

Begin planning a route around campus by identifying the location of each room on the class schedule. In the weeks prior to the start of school, class schedules are distributed, either by mail or at a school-wide orientation session. Most class schedules contain a list of teachers and room numbers for the typical school day.

Find ten minutes to sit with your child and sift through the orientation materials for a school map. With this map and the class schedule in hand, highlight the following locations:

- Classes one to six (or seven), including P.E.
- Locker
- School cafeteria and where the lunch line begins
- Bathrooms
- Main office—where the principal, vice principal(s), and counselors live
- Pickup and drop-off location (either the bus stop or a mutually agreed upon location where these exchanges will occur)

During orientation, teachers and staff members will introduce new students to the school campus through a series of activities. Remembering the location of six or more classrooms may be low on your child's priority scale compared to socializing with friends, so consider visiting the school in the evening hours with your child to get a better idea of where to locate each of the highlighted areas from your mapping activity. After a brief trip around the campus, consider challenging your child with the following scavenger hunt.

Scavenger hunt

This activity will give your child a better sense of how long it takes to move from class to class during the day. Becoming more familiar with the school campus also decreases the possibility of getting lost on the first day. The summer months provide an ideal opportunity to visit the school campus. As your child traverses the corridors with a map in hand, he begins to form a mental picture of the school's layout. Prior to the summer break, stop by the school's front office and request a map. Inquire about any times when the school may be closed or inaccessible. Typically, schools close their doors and prohibit access to the campus for at least one month during the summer break. Opt to explore the campus in the weeks immediately preceding the return to school; your child is more likely to focus on the details of your trip then—and to remember them later.

The parent's role in the scavenger hunt is to provide transportation to and from the school site. Beyond the free shuttle service, you may also offer to hold the stopwatch and record notes on the activity sheet. Follow your child's lead as to how much assistance to offer. If she decides to invite a friend along, you can offer to record times for both kids; if you sense impending embarrassment, just let them know you will wait at the front of the school for them to complete the activity. Take a few moments to tour the campus on your own. Note the location of the front office. Ideally, your visits with the staff inside will be limited to positive discussions.

Scavenger hunt materials:
- Class schedule
- Watch or stopwatch
- Piece of paper
- Pen

★ COACHING TIP

When selecting a drop-off and pickup location, steer clear of the area immediately in front of the school. Opt instead for the parking lot entrance where you can avoid the unpleasantness of car horns and gestures that can put a damper on your day.

With a stopwatch in hand (unless the parent is handling this), record the start time on the activity sheet, then proceed to the first destination on the list that follows.

After arriving at the locker, open it before recording the travel time in the area labeled "Drop-off spot to locker." Shut the locker and continue traveling from location to location, using the record below as a guide.

START LOCATION	START TIME	ROUTE TRAVEL TIME
Drop-off spot (bus stop or parent drop-off spot) to locker:		
Locker to class #1:		
Class #1 to class #2:		
Class #2 to locker:		
Locker to class #3:		
Class #3 to class #4:		
Class #4 to class #5:		
Class #5 to locker:		
Locker to class #6:		
Class #6 to class #7 (if you have 7 classes):		
Last class to locker:		
Locker to pickup location (bus stop or parent pickup spot):		

Before admiring the total travel time, add an extra minute to each of the recorded travel times. Why? With potentially hundreds of other students crowding the halls, travel time will increase. Were any of the recorded travel times longer than four minutes? If so, suggest a few of the following time-saver tips.

Minimize locker trips. Rather than visiting the locker after every other class, limit restocking trips to times when the locker is conveniently located on the path to a class. Taking books for two or three classes may be a more efficient option, especially when the classrooms are close together.

Plan ahead. Encourage your child to leave school with the supplies she will need for first period the following day. The morning hours can be unpredictable. Showing up late to first period is a tough way to start the day, particularly for the child who already struggles to get out of bed in the morning.

Avoid restroom repeats. It may not be realistic to expect to use the restroom and visit the locker in the same passing period. Although at times your child won't be able to avoid the need to visit both spots, suggest saving restroom trips for longer breaks (snack break, lunch, and before P.E.).

As your child becomes more comfortable with middle school, you may notice an increased desire for independence—excluding, of course, the need for continued chauffeur service and the occasional request for funds. The influence of peers and the new middle school environment triggers change in adolescents. Within a few weeks of your child's starting school, you may notice a host of new personality traits cropping up. When you ask about homework, the typical middle schooler response is, "I've got it handled" or "I finished it all at school." Kids are trying on their new role as aspiring, independent teens, which simply means they don't want help with anything that might make them look like a younger child, dependent on Mom and Dad. Middle schoolers are looking to make a clean break from the helping hands of their parents in nearly every area of their lives, from homework to social planning. As difficult as this sudden shift in persona can be for you as a parent, take comfort in the thought that, in time, your child will face challenges for which your ideas will be welcomed once again. Acknowledging the changes in your child's life as well as the need to shift your parenting mind-set can prevent hours of unnecessary frustration for you both. Although at times it may seem as though your child no longer wants you close by, it's important to remember that she still needs you to fill a significant role in her life. Adolescents learn how to thrive through support and ongoing encouragement from parents. Without this critical piece in place, the emotional puzzle of adolescence can become overwhelming for kids. There's more to come in the following chapters on the topic of independence and the changing role of parents. But before moving our focus away from the school campus, there are a few additional quirks about the middle school day worth mentioning.

★ COACHING TIP

Arriving after the bell rings equates to being tardy in most middle school classrooms. Too many tardies may lower a student's final grade. Review the student handbook and individual class syllabi with your child so you're well informed about each teacher's policy on this issue. Set up a regular interval for your child to check in with each teacher to confirm how many tardies and absences they have recorded. If there are any disagreements, work with your child to clear them up prior to the arrival of the quarterly report card.

Anxiety over physical education

During the elementary school years, P.E. was probably a welcome relief from an otherwise steady diet of reading, writing, and math. In most cases a student's achievement was measured by her effort and a change of clothes wasn't required. The transition to a physical education period with a certified athletic instructor can be a startling addition to the middle school day. Teachers expect students to don a uniform *and* complete a series of written assignments *and* display exemplary effort during the physical challenges of each P.E. session. With the exception of a few schools that provide exemptions for students already involved in an athletic sport, most students will be expected to include P.E. class as a part of their schedule. And yes, the class will be graded.

Is someone staring at me?

Most schools require students to change into school-issued uniforms. And yes, changing in the locker room with a complete group of strangers is part of the fun associated with middle school. The good news is that everyone feels equally uncomfortable as they scramble to get dressed. If changing makes your child feel uncomfortable, consider sharing a few of the following suggestions.

Start a conversation by asking, "Are you nervous about changing for P.E.?" If that question stirs feelings of anxiety, consider asking a second question, "Have you thought about wearing part of your uniform under your regular clothes?" If the Superman method of clothes swapping is not an option, discuss the possibility of finding a bathroom stall where changing might be a more private affair. Unfortunately, most locker rooms don't come equipped with enough stalls to accommodate everyone. Although the first few weeks may feel awkward, the initial shock of changing in front of a group of strangers wears off. Encourage your child to hang in there for a few weeks until the anxiety subsides.

What's that smell?

P.E. uniforms tend to show signs of wear and tear by mid-year. Having a second set benefits you and your child—particularly when the first set misses its weekly trip to the washer. The extra set also comes in handy if the first set goes MIA. Washing a P.E. uniform takes minimal effort. Consider handing over the responsibility for this task to your child from day one. The consequences of having a smelly gym suit will provide plenty of motivation for learning this simple procedure.

★ **COACHING TIP**

Look for opportunities throughout the year that allow your child to practice independence and the responsibility that comes along with it. Learning to care for their personal belongings is one obvious element of the move toward independence.

Study strategies for tackling homework

Assuming responsibility for meeting a teacher's expectations doesn't end when the last bell rings. Eventually, all students come face-to-face with a healthy portion of study time in the after-school hours. Completing those assignments can keep students working late into the night. Wouldn't it be wonderful to know that all of your child's homework was completed before the midnight hour?

The reality of middle school for many kids is a struggle to manage their workload and the expectations of multiple teachers. The transition from elementary school, with one teacher and one classroom, to multiple classes and teachers creates a plethora of paperwork and increased pressure to stay organized.

Designating a consistent time for homework can add to the homework challenge. Many families' schedules don't allow them the luxury of eating dinner every night at 6:00 P.M. followed by a few hours of uninterrupted homework time. If your child's after-school schedule varies, the homework schedule may need to vary as well. But the goal is to create a schedule and stick to it as often as possible. Recent research suggests that students who study in the same location for a consistent amount of time show far greater academic growth than students who continually vary both their study schedule and location. With a schedule in place and a consistent spot to get things done, the foundation is in place for efficient evening study sessions.

If the sight of your child staring blankly at a pile of textbooks raises your blood pressure, then consider trying the following four steps for successful study time. Getting started can stymie the most diligent of students unless there is a plan in place. Sit with your child the first few times you try this set of strategies. Remember that although creating a list and prioritizing tasks may be second nature to most adults, adolescents may need a few guided practice sessions with an adult before they can use the strategies effectively. Steps one through three are designed to pave the way for an efficient study process that naturally guides a child into completing nightly homework. When your child reaches step four, he will already be well on the way to completing his homework.

1. **Create a list.** A student's homework planner is a wonderful resource to record assignments and due dates, but it doesn't guarantee that any of the work will get completed. Ask your child to create a numbered list of assignments on a blank piece of paper, using the homework planner as a guide.

   In addition to the assignments that are due the following day, ask your child to add any long-term projects or tests to the list. Generating a to-do list creates a mental picture of what needs to be done by defining a specific number of tasks.

2. **Prioritize.** Parents and kids often disagree when it comes to prioritizing the activities in their lives. Homework assignments are no different from other activities. The goal of this step is to define a starting point. Let your child decide which assignment gets the top spot on the list. Ask your child to write a number next to each assignment on the list. Prioritizing brings a child one step closer to completing the tasks on her list.

3. **Estimate.** Without an estimate of how long each task will take to complete, the evening hours can quickly slip away. In the area after each listed item, ask your child to record an estimate of the time she expects to spend completing that item.

Initial estimates may be dramatically different than the actual time required to complete each item. After a few months, kids become amazingly accurate in their ability to estimate.

Parents can easily overcoach this step of the process, so try to refrain from leading questions, like "Do you really think it will take that long?" or "I bet you can finish that assignment in less time, don't you?" that deprive your child of the natural learning process. Developing an internal sense of time takes practice.

4. **Begin.** Steps one to three can take upward of fifteen minutes to complete during the first few weeks of school. However, with consistent practice most middle schoolers can complete these three steps and be ready to move to step four in five minutes or less. Beginning with the highest priority item on the list, encourage your child to work steadily in twenty-minute time blocks. At the conclusion of each study block he should get a five-minute break. As a child begins to focus for longer periods of time, the study block should be increased in five-minute increments. Rarely can middle school students study for longer than thirty-five minutes without losing focus.

Keeping study blocks short helps to improve a child's focus. With a defined work period and study break to look forward to, children tend to stay more motivated than when they are asked to work for an unstructured amount of time.

★ COACHING TIP

Using a timer for both the study and break periods can help to keep study sessions moving forward. The child may use her break periods for any activity she chooses. Five-minute study breaks give kids enough time to send a few text messages, make a short phone call, or dig into a favorite snack.

"Max is doing great as far as we can tell. He loves doing homework the way you suggested, taking breaks from time to time and then diving back into it. He proudly showed us how to look up his grades online on the school's website."

—Jenny, first-time middle school mom, Reno, NV

The first month of school is a trial period for measuring the success of homework procedures and organization strategies. Before the first progress report arrives, talk with your child about which study strategies are working and which ones need to be changed. Allow your child to propose any needed adjustments before jumping in with suggestions. In this discussion you provide guidance without assuming responsibility for your child's progress. By abandoning or adapting ineffective strategies prior to the progress report, your child will have plenty of time for improvement before the first official report card arrives.

Creating a plan for conquering homework headaches can help to smooth the path to a more enjoyable year. Occasionally, though, kids encounter academic challenges that cannot be overcome through a simple change in study strategies.

★ COACHING TIP

Alternating blocks of study time with short breaks gives parents a chance to drop in with favorite snacks. If eating in the study area isn't an option, consider placing a basket of snack options on the kitchen table.

Proactive problem-solving with your child

It takes time to adapt to a new learning environment. Change threatens a child's sense of stability. Overcoming the challenges associated with change is easier for some kids than it is for others. Typically, a child will stop complaining about assignments, teacher personalities, and minimal time with friends after the first week or two of the new middle school year. The routine of moving from class to class starts to gel, and most kids adapt to their unfamiliar surroundings. If problems persist beyond the opening weeks of a new semester, it's time for a conversation with your child. The longer a child harbors feelings of unhappiness, the greater effect these feelings will have on his ability to achieve.

Coaching a child through the problem-solving process can be a difficult transition for parents. After years of assuming the problem-solver role, you may naturally feel uncomfortable transferring ownership of this responsibility. But if you don't give your child an opportunity to practice searching for solutions, she will develop a growing dependency on others to remove the unhappiness in her life. Beginning with everyday dilemmas can ease the transition for both of you.

Common concerns of middle school children fall into three categories: peers, teachers, and workload. In each case, children should be actively involved in brainstorming solutions when concerns arise. The parent's role is to guide the problem-solving process. It's not easy to differentiate concerns that warrant a call to the school from those that require a simple shift in perception. However, often all you need to do to help resolve most problems is to listen to your child nonjudgmentally.

Set aside some uninterrupted time when you can sit with your child and listen to his list of concerns. Record each statement on a piece of paper so there is an accurate account of what was shared. After the list is complete, read each item aloud. Make any needed adjustments to the original statements before moving ahead.

Brainstorm. Very few children instinctively take action that would help to remove the barriers in their lives. Most children have learned that complaining is the swiftest way to resolution. The young child who doesn't want to eat his dinner and then complains repeatedly until his parents serve him what he wants has learned that complaining solves problems. Gradually these tactics find their way into every unpleasant situation the child confronts.

Without someone to listen to the complaints, though, a child is forced to adopt a new set of strategies.

The next time your child attempts to blast you with his or her latest complaint list, shift the focus to brainstorming a list of positive actions that have potential for positive results. The child who complains about having too little time to spend with friends can be encouraged to create a list of activities for outside the school day, when social events are easier to schedule. Teachers can also become the target of unjust accusations. If you keep the conversation moving toward action-oriented ideas, your child can learn a valuable new strategy for solving problems.

Initiate action. Brainstorming is a positive step toward becoming an independent problem-solver. However, merely assembling a list of possibilities doesn't necessarily result in action that leads to resolution. Although a parent's prodding can motivate a child to take action, this does not promote an increased sense of independence. Opt instead for sharing experiences from your life, demonstrating actions you took that led to resolution. By modeling how you moved from idea to action, you send a powerful message to your child about the value of initiating action.

Celebrate resolution. It's truly amazing to witness children gaining independence in their ability to tackle life's challenges. Moving through the problem-solving steps takes practice and patience, particularly for parents who are exploring this process for the first time with their child. As the child experiments with taking action, parents can continue their coaching role by acknowledging and celebrating progress. Statements such as "You completed all of your assignments" or "Your effort tonight was amazing" can act as powerful motivators for the child who struggles to complete nightly homework.

Occasionally, problems persist despite a child's best effort to seek resolution. Peer issues like bullying and exclusion need immediate attention and intervention from parents. In chapter 1, we examined the causes of bullying and exclusion as well as strategies for bringing these activities to an end. Before you schedule a meeting with the school counselor and principal, try revisiting these ideas; they may help you facilitate a resolution to most serious peer issues.

Children also experience challenges outside the social realm that can negatively affect their development. When a child receives failing grades after continued attempts to learn the course material, it may be a sign that either the content is too difficult or the child needs to learn it in another way. In contrast, some children sail through nightly assignments and tests with little effort. Strive to strike a balance between challenge and boredom. When the balance becomes skewed too far in either direction, it's time to sit down with your child's teachers and counselors.

Children learn in different ways. Identifying a child's learning style can help to explain why he may be struggling to learn. Most teachers now address individual learning styles by using a set of multimodal instructional strategies. Children who learn primarily by listening gain understanding through discussions and lectures. Visual learners benefit from computer-based presentations and the addition of pictures, graphs, and maps whose inclusion supports the content. Science classes give kinesthetic learners the greatest opportunity to use their learning strength through hands-on experiments.

At times, a teacher's presentation style is a complete mismatch with a child's learning style. An English class taught mainly in lecture format will cause difficulty for a child who learns primarily through discussion and interaction. In most cases, teachers accommodate different learning styles by giving the students strategies that use their learning strengths. If learning is still a struggle after talking with the teacher, your next step should be to meet with the school counselor.

In preparation for meeting with your child's teachers and the school counselor, identify your concerns and the steps you have taken to assist your child. Counselors' time is limited, given the large number of students they see on a daily basis. Teachers have very few breaks during normal school hours, so if you would like the teacher's input, suggest scheduling the meeting after the school day. The more minds you have involved, the more ideas you can generate. Idea generation is the goal of your meeting, so try to include teachers whenever possible.

Meeting with your child and the school's academic team can pave the way to a smoother year. The first progress report typically arrives between weeks four and six. Although the report is an informal account, it indicates a general pattern of progress that correlates closely with the grades you should expect to see on the quarterly report card. If you suspect that your child is struggling, don't hesitate to call the school and request a meeting. If you wait until the first quarter report card arrives, it is too late to consider taking action. Ideally, changes in your child's learning routine should take place in the weeks following the first progress report. During the fall, children build routines (both productive and unproductive) that they will be reluctant to change. This resistance can make it hard to build new routines. By adding a new member to your child's academic team, you can stimulate positive change.

Can a tutor help?

The short answer is yes, under the right circumstances. Consider tutoring if you encounter any of the following situations:

1. Your child has an extended absence from a class in which critical learning objectives were discussed.

2. Your child shows repeated signs of declining performance on assignments, tests, and projects.

3. Your child will miss a week or more of school due to a family trip or extracurricular commitment.

4. You hear your child make any of the following statements on a regular basis: "I don't understand what the teacher is talking about," "I can't remember anything we learn in class," or "No matter how hard I study, I still fail the tests."

Hiring a tutor is *not* an effective solution in any of the following situations:

1. Following the first low grade on an assignment, test, or project. Don't jump the gun and assume the rest of the quarter will continue to produce poor results. The first few weeks of school require adjustments and some time to get acquainted with teachers and curriculum. Offer to help your child study for tests or complete assignments.

2. After the first few weeks of school when your child complains, "This class is too hard," "The teacher doesn't like me," "I tried but I just don't get it," or "I understand the homework; I just don't do well on the tests." Again, kids need time to adjust to their new surroundings. Support your child's transition to her new academic environment by having her review upcoming assignment due dates and the study plan for tests. Often kids need the security of knowing they have a plan to complete homework and study effectively for tests.

3. Your child misses less than a week of school due to illness or an extracurricular commitment. When students miss less than a week of school, generally their teachers will provide a summary of the missed information. With the exception of a few advanced-level classes, most students can recover from missing less than a week of school by meeting privately with their teachers. They can also exchange emails with their teachers to ask questions about missed content if after-school hours don't permit time for a face-to-face meeting. Check in with your child's teachers after she returns to school to confirm that all missed work has been submitted.

Not all tutors are equal

If your budget will allow for the additional expense of a one-on-one tutoring experience, don't hesitate to take this route. Rather than tacking on unnecessary driving time to a tutoring center, look for a tutor who will come to your home for a one-hour session. Working individually with a tutor gives a child the opportunity to ask in-depth questions, practice new skills, and receive immediate feedback about his progress. Learning in a familiar study space gives your child access to his regular set of supplies and allows for a more focused use of his learning time.

It's fine to start by calling a friend for a recommendation; however, resist the temptation to move forward with a referral before you've made a personal review of the tutor's qualifications.

Teaching experience. Look for an adult with a history of teaching or tutoring experience. Students learn in a variety of ways. Understanding learning styles and how to present information that accommodates for learning differences is critical to comprehending challenging content.

Subject-specific expertise. Tutoring for advanced math, science, and English classes may require the experience of a subject matter expert. College students majoring in a specific field can be great tutors if they can explain the concepts in kid-friendly vocabulary.

Reliability and consistency. Ask for a few references from past clients. Inquire about the tutor's reliability in maintaining a consistent schedule for tutoring sessions. You may find it hard to reschedule a missed session within a busy after-school schedule.

What do tutors charge? The range is wide; you could pay anywhere from $20 to $100 per hour for a one-on-one tutoring session. College students tend to fall on the lower end of the pay scale, whereas teachers with advanced degrees will expect payment on the higher end. Remember, tutoring should remain a short-term endeavor, so think twice before trading experience for affordability.

In the coming chapter we leave academics to examine a realm of great interest for many middle schoolers: extracurricular activities. Athletic teams, volunteer events, and school clubs are a few of the many options that middle schoolers can add to their schedule. Our goal will be to create a sustainable plan for both you and your middle schooler that balances extracurricular goals with academic aspirations.

CHAPTER 4

Achieving Balance between School and Activities

HAVING EXPLORED the academic challenges facing your child, we now turn our focus to another equally challenging, but highly engaging area of middle school life—extracurricular activities. Kids enter middle school from various points along the extracurricular spectrum. For some children, middle school may be the first time they have engaged in an after-school pursuit; for others, the addition of another activity to an already full schedule could tip the balance from enjoyment to stress. Athletes and kids with a long-standing commitment to the arts often struggle to maintain balance in their academic and extracurricular lives. Learning how to explore new interests while managing the ongoing demands of middle school academics takes time and patience. Many adults still wrestle with maintaining balance in their personal and professional lives, so imagine the challenge our kids face while trying to do the same. Yet whether your child is new to the idea of after-school activities or a seasoned veteran, participating in something new can open fresh opportunities to explore interests and build friendships. Again, the key is finding the right balance.

Planning a balanced schedule is not that difficult; with the help of a few guidelines, you can coach your child as she creates an appropriate blend of activities and academic courses. That's the easy part. It's the actual implementation of what you have planned that takes effort, consistency, and persistence. Participating in a variety of school activities while striving to achieve in class can leave kids feeling stretched. It's important to remember that each child is unique with respect to the number of activities and expectations that he or she can commit to without becoming overextended. Creating a plan in advance of the school year can limit the number of conflicting extracurricular events while still enabling your child to explore new opportunities.

The planning process is one that parents and kids can work through together. All too often kids and parents plan separately; this leaves them at odds when it comes to fulfilling the chosen commitments. If you give children complete autonomy in the decision-making process, you run the risk that they may opt to take on either too much or nothing at all. Kids with an appetite for activity may want to try more than they can really handle; those who are more introverted may want to steer clear of any social commitments outside school hours. Parents, on the other hand, tend to err on the side of overcommitting their child to a schedule of activities, without accurately gauging the child's level of interest or ability to take on more responsibility. The result in either scenario can be an awkward mismatch of activities that leaves both kids and parents frustrated.

During the elementary years your unsolicited attempts at scheduling may have met little resistance from your child. Soccer kept kids busy through the fall. Basketball, hockey, or dance classes were staples during the winter months. Baseball opened the spring season. But middle school kids want more control over the scheduling process, particularly when it means dedicating more time and effort out of an already busy day. At this age, children are also keenly aware of the need for social time with friends. Assuming that last year's routine is still agreeable without consulting your child is a mistake.

An intermediate step on the way to relinquishing full responsibility for scheduling your child's after-school life is to work together toward building a balanced schedule. Coaching your child through the scheduling process allows you to encourage and suggest ideas while acknowledging the interests and activities your child would genuinely like to pursue. Many parents learn a lot about their child during this process. And at a time when kids generally are not very talkative, this extra insight may be a godsend. Although your child may prefer complete autonomy as she sorts through the planning process, she still needs your guidance.

Planning for a balanced schedule

Does your child's current schedule inspire enthusiasm and excitement or does the weekly calendar leave her feeling exhausted and short-tempered by week's end? Kids depend on parents to accurately gauge their ability to meet the academic demands of middle school while leaving them time to pursue new and interesting extracurricular interests. Kids don't like struggling through week after week trying to fulfill an endless slate of responsibilities. The burden on parents can also become tiring after a few weeks of shuttling their kids back and forth to after-school commitments while battling with nightly homework assignments. But choosing to opt out of all activities in favor of sitting in front of the TV every night has equally negative consequences. Opt instead for a "win-win" plan whereby both you and your child feel excited, but not overwhelmed, about the year ahead.

The first step in building a balanced schedule is to create an accurate picture of your child's current commitments. This gives you a baseline for the planning process. Find a time when you can share ten to twenty uninterrupted minutes with your child. Together, create a list of activities or commitments that currently occupy the after-school hours. Include sports practices, art classes, volunteering, or hobbies that occur on a regular basis.

Your goal is to create an accurate picture of how busy your child is today so that you can anticipate a manageable level of activity tomorrow.

★ COACHING TIP

If your child's after-school schedule has her moving somewhere different every day, consider plotting events on a desktop calendar. Events laid out on a calendar can be a vivid representation of just how busy your child's life has become. One family, frazzled from their continued scheduling conflicts, decided to use color-coded sticky notes to denote each family member's activities. Conflicting events were immediately visible, as was the very graphic image of how busy their family had become.

With an accurate picture of the current commitment load, take a moment to check in with your child. Staring at a lengthy list or full calendar of activities can be disheartening for kids, particularly when you are headed into a discussion about adding more to their plate. If your child responds to the current tally of commitments with a look of bewilderment or an exhausted sigh, consider prioritizing the activities on your list. You could replace the lowest-priority with something new to try in the coming year; this will likely be a welcome relief for the child who has been caught in the doldrums of a routinely rigorous schedule.

★ COACHING TIP

Parents have the power to guide the exploration of new interests that grow into lifelong passionate pursuits. Yet you should take care not to push your child to take on an auxiliary list of activities that you believe to be wonderful but your child couldn't care less about. Guide, but leave room to be guided by your child as he explores the world and its many opportunities.

Some families experience the exact opposite of an overplanned schedule—nothing appears on the calendar. What do you do if your list is empty? Your child's nonschool hours may be devoid of scheduled activity, and that can be OK. Organized sports and specialized activities require a significant investment of time and money that many families cannot afford. Yet it can be an intimidating challenge (for some kids as well as parents) to stir yourself from a habit of chronic inactivity to explore a more active lifestyle. Consider local community service organizations or volunteer opportunities that appreciate an extra hand from time to time. Having the flexibility to drop in may eventually expand your child's interest into a regular commitment.

★ COACHING TIP

Watch out! It's easy for kids to become too busy. A recent study conducted by researchers at Columbia University found that seven out of ten kids experienced stress on a daily basis. For many kids, middle school marks a shift toward becoming more socially active. But keep in mind that it's essential for a child's growth and well-being to leave room in his weekly schedule for unstructured time with friends.

Having made an accurate accounting of your child's current commitments, turn your attention to the gamut of extracurricular choices middle school has to offer. A list of common, school-sponsored activities appears in the next section. Review your school handbook or website for a specific list of activities. Typically, these resources will also have a basic description of the activities, including the duration of the commitment that kids are expected to fulfill. As you and your child scan the list of potential offerings, consider looking for a few activities that may coincide with your child's current interests but not be directly related to them. For example, chess club members are often avid computer fans. Engaging in a one-on-one competition with someone while learning basic strategies is similar to the attraction kids experience while playing games online. The yearbook or news club can be a likely outlet for enthusiastic writers and photographers to exercise their passion. At this point in the planning process every activity should be open to discussion and further exploration. Aim to create a list of three to five school-sponsored activities that your child would like to learn more about in the weeks prior to the school year.

> *"There were so many activities to choose from when I started middle school. I made the mistake of signing up for too many things and then missing commitments before finally having to quit a few of them when my grades went down."*
> —Sam, eighth grade student, Palatine, IL

> *"My daughter is the classic overachiever. She wants to be involved in everything. Helping her find a healthy balance where she could feel successful in school as well as in her extracurricular life was a real challenge."* —Sarah, middle school mom, Las Vegas, NV

> *"I really struggled with my child's extracurricular involvement. He didn't want to do anything except sit in front of the computer after school. It wasn't until we started looking at activities out in the community that he was willing to trade a few hours of computer time for time outside."* —Jenna, seventh grade parent, San Diego, CA

★ COACHING TIP

Most schools offer a smorgasbord of after-school activities for kids to pursue. Some kids, however, need or want a change of venue after the school bell rings. Consider looking for activities in the community. Try checking the city's recreation calendar or a newspaper listing for local volunteering opportunities.

Common school-sponsored activities

Activities vary from school to school, but most middle schools will offer a healthy menu of both athletic and nonathletic options for kids. Here are a few of the more common activities as well as a short description of each. Give the following list to your child to peruse.

Language Clubs: These clubs are great for meeting new people. Whether it's your first time learning to speak a new language or the third, language clubs give kids a time and place to talk and build friendships. Language clubs are focused on talking and learning more about the culture that surrounds the language. This type of club is likely to host field trips to local restaurants and community centers, both great opportunities for gaining cultural awareness.

Yearbook: The end of a school year signals the arrival of yearbooks. Most people don't know about the year-long commitment required of a dedicated group of kids who work to collect the pictures and stories that fill its pages. Although many schools send their yearbooks to a printing company when it comes time to assemble and print the books, the majority of the year is spent by students attending school events, gathering photos, and designing the pages. Kids interested in writing, drawing, or photography will enjoy this high-energy club.

School Newspaper: If writing, reporting, or even reading the news sounds exciting, the school newspaper would be an ideal group to join. Newspapers need a lot of students to fill a variety of different positions. Editors, reporters, photographers, and comic writers are among the many jobs on a newspaper's staff. Meeting new friends will come easily in this fast-paced club.

Live News Reporting: In place of printed newspapers, some schools now offer live TV news. The school news comes to students directly from an on-campus recording studio. Video cameras, microphones, and sound editing tools provide additional opportunities for students to join this activity. The focus on computers and movie-making software programs makes this a natural fit for kids interested in technology.

Chess Club: Board games and checkers may have sparked interest during the elementary years, but in chess club strategy takes game-playing to a new level. Chess clubs invite participation from all player levels—novice through advanced. Often chess club members are few in number, but grow to become great friends as well as competitors. Traveling to local tournaments or hosting a tournament can add to the commitment level for club members and inspire camaraderie and excitement as well.

Drama Club: Actors, singers, and dancers will find the drama club is a natural fit for their passion in the arts. Most drama clubs schedule one or two performances each year. Kids experience all areas of theater, from acting on stage to creating sets and choreographing dance moves. Trips to local theater performances as well as meeting actors and actresses may also be a part of the drama club experience. As opening night approaches, club members should be prepared for an extensive time commitment. Evening and weekend rehearsals will be added to the after-school schedule in the weeks leading up to the performance. Participation in this extracurricular club generally lasts all year; some acting roles require auditions.

National Junior Honor Society: Like its high school counterpart, participation in the junior honor society is based on academic grades, citizenship, community service, and participation in additional school activities. The general requirements for admission to this organization can be found at www.nhs.us. Schools have some flexibility in the structure of their National Junior Honor Society program, so review the school handbook for a more specific description and detailed membership requirements. Although membership in the junior level organization doesn't guarantee admittance at the high school level, most kids enjoy the challenge of excelling in a variety of areas and consequently receive invitations to the National Honor Society.

Band: Music lovers who enjoy sharing their talent will find a group of lifelong friends in the school band program. In addition to after-school performances, band members also add another class to their daily schedule, which adds more time to what could already be a busy school day. Band classes are typically slotted either early in the morning or as the last class of the day. Tryouts for the school band may happen as often as twice a year; however, incoming middle school students typically participate in spring tryouts for the coming year. Fall band classes are typically limited to students who have either been admitted through a tryout or demonstrated prior musical experience.

Academic Teams: Math and science wizards are often drawn to competitions like the school science fair and math super bowl. Middle school offers a host of new opportunities to challenge a student's academic knowledge. Connecting with those who have similar interests never hurts, either.

Sports Teams: The range of athletics offered by your middle school will vary depending on the season, climate, and size of the school population. Densely populated areas in the more temperate climate zones have the luxury of offering sports activities to their students nearly year-round. In contrast, schools with a smaller number of students may field a single team in a limited number of sports. If you already participate on an athletic team outside of school, review your practice and game schedules before trying out for the school team. Players and coaches from both teams will want to know when you have scheduling conflicts. Stretching yourself to meet the expectations of two teams inevitably means a scheduling conflict, forcing you to decide which team activity to miss. Making your priorities known to both teams is an important part of taking responsibility for your participation. You can also consider taking a break from your off-campus team to play for the school team. A temporary break from the routine of regular competition can give you a chance to reconnect with school friends.

If the list of available options doesn't spark your child's interest, suggest that he band together with a group of friends and create a club of his own. New clubs crop up every year, often in response to the shared interest of a small group of excited kids. Many of the recent additions to your school's slate of activities were most likely created by students. Here are a few examples of student-created clubs and activities: ping pong club, readers and writers club, builder's club, tech club, and anime club. You can support your child's effort and interests by contacting the school to inquire about the rules for starting a new extracurricular activity.

Community service: connecting for a cause

Handling the regular routine of classes and assignments can quickly deplete a child of the energy needed to participate in any additional on-campus activities. Yet your child may find that venturing out into the community in search of volunteer opportunities provides a good break from the rigor of a challenging academic day. Volunteering often spawns mentoring relationships that benefit kids who respond to personal attention from caring adults. Talking with the elderly, serving food at the homeless shelter, or bagging groceries at the local farmers' market are a few of the many community service activities available to middle school students. Volunteering time at most community organizations or events qualifies as *community service*—a requirement at many middle schools and high schools. Interning at a local business is another way to lend a helping hand while gaining valuable experience in a niche your child may truly enjoy. Members of the National Junior Honor Society spend a healthy number of hours volunteering in the community. So consult the National Junior Honor Society school advisor if your quest for quality volunteering opportunities comes up short. Better yet, point your child in the direction of the school advisor, who may be more inspirational in her pitch for the benefits of volunteering. Building a habit of volunteering can ease the transition into the high school years when kids are typically required to fulfill a minimum commitment of sixty community service hours over the course of a school year.

Beyond fulfilling a school or club requirement, volunteering brings people closer together in the community. Check the newspaper for a calendar of local events. Most community events depend on volunteers and would be happy to have a group of energetic students for an afternoon. Consider encouraging your child to invite a group of friends to share an afternoon together volunteering. The lure of spending more time with friends may be enough to spur the group to action.

Considering club sports?

The time commitment required by most extracurricular activities will claim a significant part of your child's afternoon hours; club sports, on the other hand, have been known to consume an entire family's availability. Before leaving the comfort of your child's recreational sports team for a club sports program, take time to thoroughly investigate the environment and commitment that club sports often require. Parents new to the notion of competitive youth athletics will find answers to commonly asked questions in the sections that follow, and veteran club parents can use these same ideas to reaffirm why their child joined a club sports program.

Club sports exist to provide a higher level of competition for children with natural athletic ability and a strong desire to compete. Soccer, basketball, and swimming are among the most popular youth club sports. However, clubs are also springing up in a variety of other sports, including baseball, hockey, water polo, and volleyball. Although some sports have a national organization that governs new club development, many of the current clubs exist because of the growing interest among parents to see their kids excel in sports.

Many kids arrive in middle school already having participated in club sports. Although the entry-level age varies from sport to sport, it's not uncommon to see kids joining developmental teams (the precursor to full-fledged club teams) as early as age five. Kids who have trouble blowing their noses and tying their shoes can now be seen traveling to compete in weekend tournaments. Often by middle school these athletic prodigies have lost interest in what was once considered a fun time with friends. In contrast, kids who wait until the middle school years to enter the realm of competitive athletics often enjoy the opportunity to bring together their talent and passion at a time when their will to compete is strongest.

Passionate and talented kids who can't be separated from the soccer ball can quickly become a challenge for the parent who wants to ensure a more balanced childhood. Club teams bring together athletes who share a common love for their sport. Watching a group of these kids engage in their passion is truly invigorating. But you need to be careful not to overload your child with additional training opportunities beyond what the team has already scheduled. Too much structure can quickly diminish a child's passion. Recent research also suggests that overtraining has become the primary cause of joint injuries and stress fractures among young athletes. Maintaining physical health and enthusiasm for sports happens naturally when kids have the opportunity to simply play in the absence of coaching or instruction. Athletes of any age delight in being able to explore their talent through unstructured play. As kids near high school age, their physical growth and continued passion for competition can trigger the desire to train on their own. Wait until your child expresses a desire to build more intensity into her training before seeking out additional practice opportunities.

Is a club program right for your child?

What is the club's philosophy? Does the club exist to develop the social and emotional sides of a child in addition to their athletic ability? As you look through the club's bylaws, scan for words like *citizenship, character,* and *academic standards.* Most club programs now seek to develop the whole child by requiring a basic level of academic achievement and a commitment to community service.

How are players selected? Although clubs hold tryouts throughout the year, many kids earn their positions through private invitation from a coach. Ask about the selection process so there are no misunderstandings.

How long is the season? Depending on the climate in your area, club sports can be limited to the traditional three-month season or run virtually year round, like soccer in the more temperate climate of California. Ask the coach or team parent for a calendar from the prior year so you will have a better understanding of just what type of commitment awaits your family in the coming year. In addition, inquire about the team's tentative list of commitments for the coming year, which should include competitions and tournaments both during and outside the traditional season calendar.

What costs are involved? The biggest shock for most parents new to the club experience is the ongoing expense. Recreational sports typically ask for a one-time registration fee that covers uniforms, supplemental insurance costs, and field maintenance fees. In contrast, when it comes to the fees you can expect to pay during your child's tenure on a club team, uniform costs are just the tip of the iceberg. Clubs choose to structure their fees and payment schedules in a variety of ways, ranging from the one-time outlay—which can be equivalent to a down payment on your next car!—to monthly installment plans covering costs in the immediate future. Fees go to fund new uniforms (two to three sets, including warm-ups), referees, league registration, tournaments (travel expenses not included), new equipment, and the coaching staff.

Ask current club parents about the tally of expenses to get a more detailed outlay of what you can expect.

Who is coaching the team? Ask about the coach's credentials, and in particular his or her experience working with kids. A coach with a professional playing career on his resume sounds great, but often these gifted athletes developed their talent without the assistance of coaching at a younger age. They simply had the ability to do what most of us must learn through the teaching process. At the younger ages and through middle school, children are still developing a mastery of basic techniques that require the expertise of a coach who can break down complex skills into smaller, easy-to-follow steps. Before you commit your child's participation to the team, attend a few practice sessions to get a clearer picture of the person who will affect your child's life on a weekly basis.

Programs with a long history and tradition of competition have a coaching hierarchy that begins with a head coach or lead trainer who oversees a cast of supporting team coaches. Team coaches in larger club programs typically shoulder the responsibility of training multiple teams. Speaking from my experience as a former soccer head coach, there were years when I trained three teams while overseeing the training regimen for the club's ten additional teams. The challenge to be present at multiple match locations on a single day often meant one team wouldn't see me. Given the possibility that your team may be left without a coach at times, it's important to inquire about the percentage of practices and competitions your coach is expected to attend and the club's policy for providing a substitute in his absence. On many occasions I stood across the field from frustrated kids and parents as they struggled to compete without a club-appointed coach. Of course, the occasional illness can interrupt a coach's full-time attendance, but you should endeavor to ensure a solid commitment from the club that a coach will be present at all competitions—your child is sacrificing a lot and deserves the same level of commitment from his coach.

In my twenty-year tenure as a club soccer coach I had the pleasure of guiding some of the nation's most gifted athletes between the ages of eight and eighteen. Among these highly talented, passionate children were many kids who would have benefited far more from the less competitive recreational environment, in which equal play time for all participants guarantees growth for the greatest number of players. As a coach my charge was to select, through tryout or personal invitation, the most gifted soccer athletes I could find within the immediate geographic area. This often meant attending local recreational matches and pitching the benefits of club soccer to parents on a weekly basis. Kids as young as eight were asked to try out for the club's youngest team—the under nine group. You might think that with a start this young these soccer prodigies were all but assured a spot on the college soccer team. In reality, many of these kids lost interest in soccer by the start of their high school years. In stark contrast to most countries, where kids play in the street or for their school teams until nearly the teen years, in the United States we have pushed our youth program to the point of fatigue for many kids. Gathering information through informal conversations with parents and direct inquiries with club members will help you decide whether a club program is the best fit for your child and your family.

Motivating the uninspired child

Are you having trouble encouraging your child's participation in extracurricular activities? Kids may shy away from joining clubs and onsite school activities for a variety of different reasons, ranging from shyness to anxiety over their perceived inability to succeed. Although participation in an activity you choose may not inspire a sudden desire to leave the house, requiring your child to take part in some type of organized activity two to three times a week promotes the healthy development of social skills and access to a new peer group.

Connecting the introverted child with a mentor-minded adult or organization creates a safe bridge between your home and the outside world. Joining an active group of peers can often be overwhelming for the child who prefers the company of one friend or a caring adult. Libraries, youth groups, and summer camp programs are staffed by adults who enjoy working with kids. During the after-school hours and summer months, middle school kids can volunteer in a variety of capacities while under the direct supervision of an adult mentor. Identifying adult mentors who relate to your child takes time and a keen eye for special people who share your values and ideals and also are able to connect with adolescents (a truly rare and valuable trait). Begin your search for mentors by connecting with teachers or the principal at your child's elementary school. Often schools partner with mentoring organizations as part of their ongoing connection with the community. Adding mentors creates a vital link in the support your child can receive during the middle school years. Counselor-in-training programs actively recruit middle school kids to staff their medley of summer camp activities. Community- and church-based youth groups also have a need for kids who would like to guide younger elementary age kids through after-school and summer programs. Assuming a leadership or supervisory role among a group of younger children removes the anxiety that many kids feel with their own peer group, and it may be just the experience your child needs to bring him out of his personal shell.

Avoiding burnout

Introverted children aren't the only ones avoiding participation in after-school activities. A growing number of our nation's most active kids are losing interest in sports, the arts, and their schoolwork as they enter the middle school years. Taking a closer look at the increased activity load that many kids have continued to maintain throughout their elementary school years, we begin to see the cause of the burnout. Take, for example, Julia, whose avid participation in soccer and the school band keeps her busy until 8:00 P.M. on weeknights, often with overlapping practices that require a quick change of clothes and dinner on the go as Mom traverses the cross-town commute to the next activity. She arrives home with little room for rest or anything resembling meaningful conversation with other family members. The push to complete homework and study for weekly tests consumes the next three hours of Julia's evening, leaving her a few minutes of down time to IM (instant message) friends and say goodnight to Mom and Dad. How many adults do you know who could withstand the rigor of a weekly schedule like Julia's?

Julia's life is characteristic of many overscheduled kids arriving in middle school today. The onslaught of activities didn't happen as a result of starting middle school. It grew steadily in response to years of continually adding more and more until the child finally reaches a point of overload. Without the skills or experience needed to manage multiple expectations, many kids find themselves exhausted from a daily routine that most adults couldn't maintain.

Where did the expanding list of opportunities come from, and why do we, as parents, feel compelled to have our children participate? One reason for the recent onslaught of activity is simply the availability of opportunities. A generation ago, organized programs for sports and specialized arts were the exception rather than the norm. In the last few decades our idyllic vision of kids playing stickball in the park has been transformed into squads of kindergartners playing sixty-game schedules of year-round baseball. From the early elementary school years, many children now have the opportunity to participate in a full menu of activities from basketball to ballet.

The myth of a potential college scholarship seems to justify the added expense and travel time many parents invest. The reality, with respect to college scholarships and professional athletics, is that less than 5 percent of high school age children receive college scholarships for either the arts or athletics. Less than 1 percent of children will achieve a professional level in either discipline. Nevertheless, competition for participation in top programs and professional coaching has driven parents to seek out and sign up for programs miles away. But for many children (and parents), the time spent engaging in these activities is time away from friends and family. Childhood, for today's generation of kids, has been redefined as a time for structured activity rather than free play.

Shifting your perception away from participation as a necessity, to participation based on your child's enthusiasm, can help bring balance to your child's extracurricular life. But moving away from what society has come to accept as the norm brings its share of challenges. Friends, both yours and your child's, may wonder why you are not as overscheduled as they appear to be. Focus on your child's enthusiasm (or lack thereof) to guide the activities on her after-school schedule.

How to measure enthusiasm

To spot a child's dwindling enthusiasm, you may need a trained eye or the help of a trusted friend who knows your child. The day-to-day routine most families maintain keeps them from seeing the subtle changes that eventually lead to huge shifts in their children's behavior. It's easy to overlook your child's grumpy attitude for a few days or her flippant comment about quitting the team after a tough practice. Many parents attribute these subtle shifts in attitude to the normal emotional changes of a moody middle schooler; when confronted with the reality that their child is burned out, they respond with disbelief and denial.

Without turning your parenting role into that of a guard imposing a series of emotional checkpoints, designate a time every two to three days when you will consciously take stock of your child's emotional state. The brief stretches of "down time"—on the drive to school, after returning home from an evening activity, or just before bedtime—often reveal a child's location along the emotional spectrum. Although occasional reluctance to attend an after-school practice isn't cause for alarm, if your child steadily refuses to participate, it is a strong signal that burnout is approaching. If he makes explicit statements like "I don't like doing this anymore" or "This isn't fun for me," you should acknowledge these with your attention and commitment to inquire further about the cause behind these feelings of discontent. Another more subtle indicator of burnout is the sudden disappearance of equipment or materials required for participation in after-school endeavors. The habitually missing baseball glove or band instrument can be attributed to something greater than a lack of responsibility. Children who are passionate about their extracurricular pursuits find the motivation to keep their gear close and prepared for their next outing. Finally, when practices or commitments fall by the wayside or your child expresses ambivalence in having missed the event, you should acknowledge the signal for a break. By checking in with your child, either through observation or conversation, you can minimize the chance of burnout while maximizing ongoing enthusiasm for thriving in the years ahead.

★ COACHING TIP

When a parent's energy to promote an activity exceeds a child's enthusiasm, it's time for a break—or at the very least a conversation about how to bring excitement back to your child's life.

Switching gears

Responding to a child's request for a break from the routine marks a monumental step in the parent–child relationship. Many parents tend to keep their children involved with a full slate of after-school activities. After two to three months of continuous activity, kids need a break. Taking a break doesn't mean lying around on the couch for the duration of the afternoon and evening hours. Breaking from the rigor of a traditionally busy schedule gives kids the opportunity to explore new interests. Participating on a school sports team could be the ideal diversion for the avid artist who needs a break from the dance studio or painter's canvas. The opposite is true for athletes. Exploring the arts can be a welcome change from spending time on the court. The key to connecting kids with new interests is identifying an environment that removes all performance-related expectations. Continually asking a child to perform at peak levels eventually leads to exhaustion and a loss of interest. Look for community-sponsored events, recreational activities, or mentoring opportunities that focus on fun. The only expectation that should be required for participation is showing up.

Whether your child's interests spawn a year-round sports commitment or a series of community service events, the middle school years are sure to be filled with a wealth of new extracurricular options. Finding places and people who connect with your child's interests is one of the most important actions you will take in the coming years.

In fulfilling the role of resource guide for your child, you may need to investigate and engage in many of your preteen's interests so that your recommendations are well informed. Chief among the long line of middle school attractions is the surge toward online interaction. YouTube, MySpace, and Facebook stand out on a growing list of web-based services popular with today's middle school kids. In the coming chapter we will dig into the world of online media in an effort to connect you with knowledge and strategies for keeping your child safe online.

CHAPTER 5

Keeping Kids Safe Online

MAINTAINING A BALANCE between school responsibilities and extra-curricular commitments is a major challenge for today's families. Another struggle for parents is negotiating a safe environment for their child's growing curiosity about the Internet. When they were that age, their neighborhood friends would drop by for an impromptu after-school get-together; that's no longer such a common practice. Today's kids are far more sophisticated in their social interactions. The move to continue friendships online, through instant messages and social networking sites, simply takes advantage of a new medium for these relationships to grow and change. The challenge to stay in sync with your child's developing internet prowess may leave you feeling bewildered and even frustrated at times. Broadening your own technological knowledge base will help to alleviate the stress and uncertainty you may feel about your child's computer-related activity. However, knowledge alone is not enough to meet the continued challenge of staying connected with your child as he becomes a savvy internet user. In this chapter you will learn a new set of strategies for tackling many of the internet-related issues facing parents of today's middle school children.

Connect, collaborate, and problem-solve

My earliest memories of sitting in front of a computer date back to the days of DOS-based systems and the Apple IIE. As a child, I was overjoyed at the thought of being able to hit the delete key, no longer needing the assistance of correction fluid or my rickety old typewriter. The evolution of the computer from word processor to worldwide communication device seemed to happen nearly overnight. In the span of two decades, the Internet grew to become the single greatest source of information our world has ever known. Shortly after the emergence of dial-up internet service came broadband (high-speed, continuously connected internet service), which brought new meaning to the word *connectivity*. The irony facing parents today is that we live in a world where transcontinental communication can be achieved in seconds, whereas staying connected with your own child takes years to accomplish.

Children born today don't know a world without computers or the Internet. Given the gap in knowledge many parents have with respect to technology, a child's online activity often escapes parents' notice or exceeds the comfort level many parents have when venturing online. This new generation of children, often called the Millennial Generation or Generation Y, comes equipped with a highly developed sense of what it means to connect, collaborate, and problem-solve using technology. Questions that formerly took weeks to answer now find solutions in minutes, if not seconds, after posting a blast to their online network. Social networking has given rise to powerhouse sites like MySpace and Facebook. Although both of these media giants cater mainly to teen users, their influence spawned the creation of Club Penguin, Webkinz, and Moshi Monsters, three sites now popular among tweens making their way through the elementary and middle school years. With the power to connect at any time and with anyone, children have the world at their fingertips.

Accessibility doesn't come without a price, though. Given the Internet's daily evolution, kids often find themselves exposed to new websites and online resources without the assistance of a qualified guide. Website addresses flow freely from one child to the next like notes handed from desk to desk. Although schools are gradually finding ways to censor inappropriate website content, their efforts do little to curb the vast amount of unchecked time kids spend online in the after-school hours. The responsibility of leading a child through the gauntlet of potentially harmful online media outlets has fallen on the shoulders of parents, many of whom remember a time when computers were nothing more than an efficient way to type a letter.

Bringing your home up to code

Every child needs a computer with internet access, right? The answer is a qualified yes. With guidance and supervision, children can learn to use the Internet to explore new worlds, engage in productive online communities, and expand their knowledge in virtually any area of interest. But without instruction, your child is at risk from a range of different threats.

A computer with internet access can either be lifesaving or life-threatening. Kids can now look online for a group of peers or a qualified teen coach as a primary source of support for battling bullies, depression, or the host of other issues that can affect a child's emotional well-being during the middle school years. At the same time, online predators and cyberbullying can put kids into life-threatening situations. Although some websites such as cybersafety.com and netsmartz.org devote themselves to the daily task of filtering through questionable content, their efforts can't stem the tide of new content. In addition to computers, cell phones now come equipped with the ability to connect to the Internet. Many of the policies you put in place regarding internet use on a computer can also carry over to your child's cell phone use.

At least one personal computer has become a standard in most U.S. homes today. The number of households with one or more computers has risen steadily over the last decade, from a mere 20 percent of homes in 1998 to a startling 75 percent by the year 2008. Kindergartners now huddle over laptops during times that were formerly reserved for Legos and Barbie dolls. In our haste to respond to societal pressure to stay technologically current, we have glossed over the importance of engaging in thoughtful discussions about how technology's latest toys will impact our lives and, in particular, the way children interact with the world. With the focus now on creating computers that are easier to use, new purchases rarely include any information beyond where to insert the power cord. Perhaps the ubiquity of personal computing among children has led computer makers to assume that kids already know their way around the Internet. Consider taking the time to create a plan for a computer's arrival or placement to maximize the chances for a safe and secure online experience.

You can provide a safe and secure environment for all internet-related activity by designating a central location for all of your family's computers. A desk or table placed strategically in either the family room or kitchen offers two benefits. In either of these high-traffic areas, parents can easily check on their child's internet activity more frequently. The ever-present possibility of your taking an occasional glance as you stroll through the family room can be enough to hold your child accountable for her time online. Bringing all of your family's computers to a centralized location has the added benefit of bringing family members together. Even though you may not hold extended conversations with your child, she still benefits from sharing the same space with you. Who knows—the close proximity may spur questions or unexpected opportunities to share something interesting, which typically doesn't happen when kids disappear behind a bedroom door. A laptop's portability adds an extra level of challenge for families who want to keep everyone working together. By clearly defining a limited area for your common computer, you can eliminate the possibility of your child sequestering the family laptop—a frequent practice among mobile teens.

Having designated a computer spot, you can turn your attention to creating an acceptable use plan for your family's time online. Most schools now require parents and kids to sign a document that defines a set of rules governing safe internet use at school. The consequences for failing to abide by the plan are also clearly articulated in this document. If a copy of this school document doesn't appear during the first few weeks of school, consider requesting one. Draw on your child's school experiences as you co-create your family's plan. As one of the main points in your plan, I suggest designating internet-free times each week when all family members will peel themselves away from the screen to engage in an alternative activity. An hour after school or a few hours during each weekend is normally enough time to ensure a clean break from the electronic umbilical cord. Commit to specific time slots each week in which all family members will surrender their electronic devices in exchange for time together.

Carving out a few hours of computer-free time still leaves a significant portion of the week when your family will scramble for their fair share of time online. Sharing computer time in a household with multiple kids and a few email-hungry adults may necessitate greater structure in your plan. By scheduling equitable amounts of time on the weekly calendar, you can alleviate the inevitable rush to commandeer a work station every evening. The imposition of a weekly schedule may not bring happiness, but it will bring some sanity to your family's computer use.

"What were you looking at?"

Bringing the structure of a schedule to your family's plan lays the groundwork for a discussion about inappropriate content. Over dinner or in another uninterrupted twenty-minute time slot, engage in a quick brainstorming activity with your family in which you create a list of types of websites that are off limits. Each family has a different idea about what constitutes inappropriate content, but most would agree that websites promoting pornography, gambling, violence, hate groups, and drug use are off-limits. Sites that you would like to view with your child prior to allowing their independent use can be marked with a PG for parental guidance. YouTube may be a site deserving of the PG rating. The entirely user-generated media site features over a million video clips spanning a variety of topics. Although the site actively removes any pornographic content users attempt to upload, a significant number of clips feature violent and questionable content.

The social networking sites Facebook and MySpace may be among your top nominees for the list of restricted sites. But resist the temptation (for the moment) to add either one to your family's list until you have read the coming sections of this chapter specifically devoted to these controversial online venues.

Safe surfing strategies

In conjunction with writing a plan for safe and secure internet use, some families also list ideas that promote safe online surfing. Consider the following five strategies for responsible internet use at home.

1. If you unknowingly stumble upon information that the family considers inappropriate, quickly click the Back button in your browser. This easy-to-develop reflex prevents 99 percent of content-related issues. If a child knows where the Back button is located there should never be questionable pictures or text information lingering on the screen.

2. If it's illegal offline, it's illegal online. Copying a music CD or downloading your friend's entire song list from his iPod can result in stiff legal penalties. Though the music industry has put precautionary measures in place to prohibit illegally sharing music, the appearance of new music and software-

sharing sites continues to cause problems. Falsifying personal information for the purpose of gaining access to age-restricted sites also qualifies as unlawful behavior.

3. Email and instant messages from strangers are cause for alarm. Saying no to strangers has become standard practice for kids today in the offline world. Yet the majority of tweens and teens think little of exchanging personal information in response to anonymous inquiries while online. Although schools are working to promote safety online, the message doesn't have nearly the effect that the "say no to strangers" campaign had over the past few decades.

4. Create an account online only when a parent is present. Email services and most social networking sites require the completion of an online form prior to creating an account. Provide only the required information (normally designated with an asterisk). Consider using a family email address if one is required to complete the account setup process. With a centralized email address you have better access to unsolicited requests or inappropriate messages that might reach your child if she had her own account.

5. Plan to spend time together online (as parent and child) so you can stay current on your child's browsing activity. Kids new to the online arena are often excited about sharing their discoveries or internet-based hobbies. Responding to your child's excited attempts at sharing gives you a brief glimpse at their online world while also acknowledging the importance of their interests. Periodic check-ins keep you engaged and aware of your child's activity in the online world in the same way you want to know their whereabouts in the offline world.

Before bringing your family's discussion to a close, spend a few moments talking about the consequences for failing to adhere to the family's plan. Children often propose extreme punishments (a year without the Internet) that do little to educate and promote healthy internet use after the punishment is lifted. Temper the severe punishment ideas with a more logical, long-term approach. Consider a healthy portion of cyber safety reading and a session with the school's computer lab specialist, who can guide your child's development of safe internet practices. Education coupled with a short respite from the Internet is often enough to reestablish an adherence to the family's mutually agreed-upon objectives.

Productive prying

Continued communication keeps kids and parents connected. Establishing a climate of trust helps to ensure an open line of communication on internet-related issues. Occasionally, though, kids stop talking or become secretive about their time online. If you suspect behavior that violates your family's acceptable use plan, ask for some one-on-one time when your child can guide you through a tour of his recent internet adventures. If your request is met with an eye roll or similar gesture of reluctance, you may need to conduct an informal search on your own time. Fortunately, your computer remembers where you go and who you see.

Internet Explorer, Safari, and Firefox are all internet browsers. Each of these programs serves as a connection point between your computer and the Internet. Like a car traveling along an endless stretch of highway, a computer's browser can deliver you to any destination (website) on the World Wide Web. But unlike the average automobile, a browser retains a history of your internet travel destinations.

Taking ten minutes to investigate your child's online activity can save you hours of needless anxiety. With your computer on and the internet browser open, look for the word "History" along the top line of your browser screen. In Internet Explorer, click "Tools" and look for History in the dropdown menu. The browser history records a detailed list of website locations the user has recently accessed. Although you can adjust the duration of your browser's history, the default setting is two weeks, giving you ample opportunity to scan for any suspicious activity. Different browsers offer different methods for clearing the browser history; if yours is not obvious, try the Help feature.

If responsible internet use continues to be a struggle, consider purchasing one of the many commercially available parent monitoring programs. With a few quick clicks parents can gain access to every instant message and email a child sends or receives from the family's computer. Unlike a browser history, a monitoring program's memory cannot be deleted by anyone except the person who originally installed it. Before you resort to this, though, sit down with your child and share your concern for his safety. Installing an internet surveillance program sends a specific message to your child: "I don't trust you." Often kids and parents can come to an agreement about the importance of safe internet use and the value of retaining an honest and trusting relationship.

Your secret decoder ring

"OMG PAW G2G" ("Oh my god, parents are watching, got to go"). Sitting next to your middle schooler as she happily clicks away on instant messages (IM) won't reveal much about her online conversations unless you learn the lingo for these often indecipherable exchanges. Unfortunately, most kids are not interested in educating their parents in the finer points of this modern-day pig Latin. Consider the following list of commonly used acronyms as a primer for learning to understand teen tech speak. You'll find a complete dictionary of online acronyms at www.teenchatdecoder .com. Tackle a few new terms each week and you will be well on your way to IMing with the best of them. Try a few of your newfound favorites in a text message to your child, and wait for her startled reply.

AUD—Are you done?
BAF—Bring a friend

BF—Boyfriend
BFF—Best friends forever

CD9—Code 9, parents are around	POTS—Parents over the shoulder
CYA—See ya	QT—Cutie
DIKU—Do I know you?	UR—You are
HHJK—Ha ha, just kidding	YWTHM—You want to hug me
KPC—Keeping parents clueless	YOYO—You're on your own

Let's connect

Amid the flurry of text messages kids send and receive, it's hard to believe that this nearly ubiquitous form of communication accounts for only a portion of their peer-to-peer communication. If you want to know where to meet a friend or the status of your social plans, you send a message. But messaging doesn't provide an efficient way to share your plans with an entire group of friends or a venue for sharing highlights of special events. A growing number of kids are extending their one-on-one and small group interactions to their entire network of friends through the use of social networking websites.

The modern-day equivalent of hanging out at your local community center, social networking now accounts for nearly 90 percent of the time kids in the twelve-to-seventeen-year-old age range spend online. Unlike the local community center that was open only during the afternoon hours and staffed with qualified adults, social networking sites draw around-the-clock participation, with a minimal amount of supervision from a virtual staff monitoring millions of users. People are free to drop in at any time either for a live conversation or to leave messages for friends to see on their next visit.

The move toward full-fledged social networking sites like Facebook and MySpace begins before a child enters middle school. Elementary school age children delight in spending hours tending to their online pets at Club Penguin, Webkinz, and Moshi Monsters. Under the guise of a fun-filled arcade, each of these sites operates a child-friendly version of social networking. Users establish a primary residence and have access to common areas, which are accessible to anyone with a user account who is currently online. What is the criterion for creating a user account? With the exception of Webkinz, which requires the purchase of a stuffed animal and registration code, nearly all of these younger social networks are free for anyone to join.

All of the kid-friendly sites have an arcade-style interface. Users are required to create an avatar (an animated figure representing the user) before participating in any of the site's features or common access environments. As the avatars navigate their way through the online world, stopping to play games and purchase trinkets, they may be contacted by any one of the other avatars currently online. The positive side to avatar-based games is they keep your child's true identity and personal information a secret. The only way to learn the identity of another avatar is by requesting it through the site's chat or message feature. Communication can arrive via either a short chat message or a note left in the avatar's mailbox. In either case, a user is free to delete the message without replying to the sender.

The downside to avatar anonymity is you never know who could be lurking around. Guiding kids to keep their true identity a secret is an essential precautionary measure that many parents wouldn't think to consider on these sites, given the playful surroundings. With some coaching and a few side-by-side sessions, you can steer your child away from unwanted encounters and toward the game areas. Given the relatively small number of users frequenting these child-friendly sites and the charge to rid online environments of predators, the online staff at each site are vigilant in their efforts to block users who demonstrate any attempt to contact children in a suspicious manner. Keeping kids safe is their primary concern. Parents are encouraged to contact website administrators if they suspect an inappropriate behavior.

The well-guarded anonymity of these sites for younger children lasts for only so long—as kids and parents eventually realize when making the transition to more mainstream social networking sites like MySpace and Facebook.

Playing with the big kids

Joining the social networking giants Facebook and MySpace now seems like little more than the next step along a predetermined path for many kids entering middle school. Although MySpace and Facebook offer many of the same features, there are distinct differences between the two services. MySpace launched its service in 2003 with a focus on sharing music by fledgling musicians who were hoping to break into the mainstream music recording industry. Little did the founders know that the company's modest mission statement would blossom into the world's largest social networking service, now connecting nearly 120 million users worldwide, with 73 million unique user accounts in the United States alone.

Facebook, by contrast, had its humble beginnings in a dorm room at Harvard University. Early in 2004, Mark Zuckerberg, one of three original founders, conceived an idea that would spread like wildfire across the Ivy League in the following year. Originally designed as a place to keep the Harvard undergrad population connected, Facebook quickly grew beyond its Ivy roots to reach colleges across the United States. Interest in this renowned new form of communication grew at an alarming rate, nearly overwhelming the small startup. In a bold move, Facebook founders made the decision to open the network to high school-age students in 2005, thus greatly expanding the network's potential user base. In the fall of 2006, just two short years after bringing their idea to the Harvard campus, Facebook's founders opened its doors to mainstream users across the United States. Membership numbers exploded into the millions, but even with its current tally of forty-three million unique accounts worldwide, Facebook membership pales in comparison to the dominant position MySpace has secured in the social networking realm.

Pressure from peers to graduate from their cuddly penguin or Webkinz pet to a Facebook or MySpace account can lead children to a critical crossroads. Legally, most children cannot participate until toward the end of their middle school years. The prevalence of underage users falsifying personal information to gain access to both MySpace and Facebook has led to widespread misuse and abuse of these sites. Although the terms of use and eligibility (which follow) stipulate the minimum age of eligibility as thirteen for Facebook users and fourteen for MySpace, many kids think very little of subtracting a few years from their birth date to meet a site's minimum age requirement.

The following text is taken directly from the Facebook Terms of Use document.

> "This Site is intended solely for users who are thirteen (13) years of age or older, and users of the Site under 18 who are currently in high school or college. Any registration by, use of or access to the Site by anyone under 13, or by anyone who is under 18 and not in high school or college, is unauthorized, unlicensed and in violation of these Terms of Use. By using the Service or the Site, you represent and warrant that you are 13 or older and in high school or college, or else that you are 18 or older, and that you agree to and to abide by all of the terms and conditions of this Agreement."

Tucked away among the long list of privileges and exclusions is the verbiage detailing Facebook's policy on membership termination:

> "The Company may terminate your membership, delete your profile and any content or information that you have posted on the Site or through any Platform Application and/or prohibit you from using or accessing the Service or the Site or any Platform Application (or any portion, aspect or feature of the Service or the Site or any Platform Application) for any reason, or no reason, at any time in its sole discretion, with or without notice, including if it believes that you are under 13, or under 18 and not in high school or college."

Also taken directly from their company's website, the following paragraph includes both the eligibility and termination information for MySpace accounts.

"Use of the MySpace Services and registration to be a Member for the MySpace Services ("Membership") is void where prohibited. By using the MySpace Services, you represent and warrant that (a) all registration information you submit is truthful and accurate; (b) you will maintain the accuracy of such information; (c) you are 14 years of age or older; and (d) your use of the MySpace Services does not violate any applicable law or regulation. Your profile may be deleted and your Membership may be terminated without warning, if we believe that you are under 14 years of age, if we believe that you are under 18 years of age and you represent yourself as 18 or older, or if we believe you are over 18 and represent yourself as under 18."

Protecting young users

Midway through 2008, both Facebook and MySpace reached agreements with attorneys general in forty-nine states (Texas declined both initiatives) to begin instituting a firmer set of policies and technology that will keep their networks free from sexual predators. Although the new call to action does little in the way of firming up their ability to track and delete underage users, the assault on predatory action was the first step that either social networking services or state governments have taken to reduce an otherwise unregulated online environment.

Pornography of any kind, including links to adult content websites and user groups created for the purpose of promoting adult content, will be removed, in accordance with the initiative's objectives. Repeated attempts at changing a user's registered age will send an alert to website administrators, triggering a thorough account review. Each of these social networking giants recognizes the significance they play in maintaining a safe environment for minors. Although they acknowledge the importance of their role in adhering to a higher standard of safety, the brunt of the responsibility for keeping kids safe on social networking sites falls on their parents' shoulders.

Though your child's first year in middle school could be free from the challenge of illegally obtaining a social networking account, you should be prepared to soon face the fury of an unrelenting thirteen-year-old who wants desperately to exercise his legal right to join his circle of friends online. Although banning your child from joining a network will limit his access at home, your hard-line tactics do little to discourage his peers' continued use of these same services. Your child's peer group will continue to exist online as it does offline even in his absence.

If you can't beat them . . .

A growing number of parents have taken the plunge into the world of social networking by creating their own accounts. On the basis of the premise that knowledge is power, parents are creating accounts in record numbers and using their online presence to meet the continued challenge of social networking misuse and abuse. Parents in the thirty-five-to-forty-four-year-old age bracket are one of the fastest-growing segments of new users outside of the twelve-to-seventeen-year-old age bracket. Overcoming the initial learning curve can be daunting, particularly given your child's fluidity with technology; however, the motivation to learn more about your child while preventing online abuse could be enough to push you past the point of fear and into action. Consider taking up temporary residence on both MySpace and Facebook. As an adult, you can register for either service in a matter of minutes. Although staying abreast of the latest teen tech trends may help bolster your confidence, keep in mind the main goal behind your presence online. For the first time, parents now have the rare opportunity to peer into their child's social network of friends, albeit from the safe distance of a computer display. Ask your child to add you to her list of online friends, but expect to be required to meet a few conditions, assuming you receive the coveted title. Tread lightly with your new friend status; you're likely to have your friend status revoked as quickly as it was granted if you post a comment on your child's profile page, ask your child about anything you saw on his profile page, or send a friend request to your child's friends.

Of course, you have the right to protect your child from content that clearly depicts violent or unsafe acts. Your child's safety overrides her right to privacy.

Creating your first account

We'll now go through the initial steps for creating a MySpace account. (Like everything on the Web, the look and feel of what we describe may change over time, but the essential elements should remain.) Facebook registration is nearly identical and should prove to be less of a challenge after you have successfully navigated the MySpace interface. Even though you'll likely be able to provide responses to all of the required registration fields in less than ten minutes, schedule a block of thirty minutes or more to allow time to explore and experiment with basic features after the signup process is complete.

With your internet browser open, go to www.myspace.com. Look for the "Sign Up" button. Click the button to bring up the account registration form. Scan the form from top to bottom, noting the variety of information you are asked to provide. There are links to the Terms of Service and Privacy Policy at the bottom of the page just above the Sign Up button. Review both documents before you complete the registration form. In addition to the eligibility and termination clause we covered earlier, you will find a plethora of information detailing specific user-related responsibilities, prohibited content, and a cautionary note about the personal information you choose to provide on your profile page.

Having read the site's disclaimers, you can complete the registration form. All fields are required except state of residence. A verification image of numbers and letters—an increasingly common security device on the Web—ensures that only human users can create an account. Before you click the final Sign Up button at the bottom of the page, check the small box confirming you have read the terms of service and privacy policy documents. Successfully navigating the registration gauntlet will bring you to the first choice in a series of options for building your profile page.

Protecting your privacy

Privacy concerns become paramount at this stage of the account setup. With the opportunity to upload a photo, kids often choose a favorite personal shot featuring friends. You also have the option of uploading a symbol instead of a personal photo or bypassing the photo option completely—in which case MySpace places the default "NO PHOTO" icon where your photo would normally appear. Clicking the "Skip this step" link will bring you to a new page where you can add friends. If you want to remain as anonymous as possible, then leave the default silhouette in place rather than adding a photo of your own. As a general rule, if you want to appear on your child's friend list, refrain from adding a picture or any other personal information that would draw attention to the fact you are a parent.

Choose your friends carefully. Adding email addresses to your friend list is the first contact point your account has with the outside world. Friends must accept invitations before their name will appear in your network. On acceptance, anyone joining your group of friends will have immediate access to your page and the information you have chosen to share. The same dynamic applies as you begin to receive and accept friend requests—often referred to as *friending*. Keeping portions of your MySpace profile private prevents unconfirmed friends from peeking at your personal information until they become official additions to your friend list.

You can adjust your privacy settings to eliminate most of the unsolicited attention you might otherwise receive. While viewing your account, look for "Privacy" at the top of the page between the words "Password" and "Spam." Click the privacy link to display a host of options for the settings associated with your account. If you take the time to review each of the areas listed on this page, you'll have a much better understanding of the features currently available on the site.

★ COACHING TIP

Neglect adjusting the privacy settings on your MySpace account, and you'll give complete access to anyone who wants to view your personal information. You can block unwanted visitors by changing the privacy setting from the default to "my friends only."

Pay particular attention to the first item on the list, "privacy." I suggest you change two particular default settings. First, under "profile viewable by," choose the "my friends only" option to keep your page hidden from everyone except your preapproved group of friends. The second, under "block users," is helpful if you continually receive unsolicited messages or friend requests. You can add these senders to a list of blocked users. Coaching your child to use both of these privacy features will significantly reduce, if not eliminate, unwelcome communication.

Next, let's peruse a few of the many features for enhancing your online presence. Both MySpace and Facebook offer similar features for users connecting and sharing information with friends in their network. We will review a few of the more prominent features, then discuss major differences between the two services.

Promoting your profile

Your user profile features personal information prominently on your page. Any hobbies, interests, or additional personal information you included during the registration process becomes part of your profile. Be careful about the items you wish to share in this section of your page. Even though uninvited guests cannot view your extended profile of personal interests and lifestyle preferences, you have no control over what your group of friends chooses to do with this information. One friend's innocent attempt at connecting you with a new acquaintance could reveal information you might have preferred to keep private. Deleting personal information removes it from the view of new visitors, but the damage may already have been done.

★ COACHING TIP

The Internet remembers everything. Guiding your child toward a safety-conscious online experience requires a routine check on the types of information she has chosen to share. Every email, photo, or comment shared online becomes public property the moment it leaves your computer.

Photo sharing

Sending a picture from your camera phone takes time and eats up valuable minutes from your monthly plan. With the photo-sharing feature now common on social networking sites, your home page can feature a collage of pictures for friends to enjoy and share. Yes, as with your profile information the pictures you choose to post become available for friends everywhere to share and alter in any way they choose. Friends viewing your photos can copy and send these images to anyone with a few clicks of the mouse. Facebook's tagging feature gives users the option to name the people in your photos. Tagging a friend sends a copy of your photo to their account. Caught up in the egocentricity of their young lives, most kids never consider the possibility that these photos could be seen by anyone other than their preapproved list of friends. Share this fact with your child; you could save her from an embarrassing moment.

"Facebook gives us the chance to create a history of what we do together. It's like a scrapbook of our teenage years."
       —*Mark, high school student, Thousand Oaks, CA*

What's new with you?

The ability to instantly update friends on your major (and minor) life events is one key power of a social networking site. Your child can connect with friends in a variety of ways. The status update feature in Facebook gives you space to include a quick note about what's new in your life. Dinner with friends, a recent movie review, or short comments on the day's events are common additions to the status update section.

However, kids rarely use the status update or blogging features that most social networking services provide; they opt instead for the creativity and connectivity of the Wall, a virtual bulletin board for comments, pictures, and video clips, now common on most sites. Friends can post messages, links to videos, or original art creations to this common area while you are away, so after you log on, take the time to check for new additions. The account owner is responsible for removing any unwanted additions.

Joining your child's social circle

Gaining access to your child's network of friends online can be nearly as challenging as it is to do offline. Parental status doesn't translate into friend status in the online world. Appealing to the website administrators won't bring you any closer to seeing what's behind the login screen, either. Privacy restrictions prevent account information from being shared between users. Your only recourse, when trying to gain access to your child's private group of friends, is to ask your child's permission. Strangely, the dynamic of trust and permission in your parent-child relationship takes a 180-degree shift when it comes to social networking.

Parents are beginning to embrace this newfound way of staying connected with their children during the middle school years. A growing number of parents are requesting friend status on their child's online network. But even for those parents fortunate enough to gain this enviable position in their child's social circle, friendship comes with a set of conditions. As one dad shared, when asked about his new online status, "I have to bite my tongue when I see my son's wall and the comments his friends choose to leave. One word of lecture from me and I lose the privilege of gaining a glimpse at what happens in his world. Short of threats and flagrantly disrespectful language, I don't say anything. I like knowing what he's doing, and I'm not willing to give that up over a few misguided comments."

At a time when kids are less than forthcoming about their social life, it is indeed a privileged position to have access to your child's daily social interactions. Never before have parents been given an opportunity to stay so close to their child's life in the way that Facebook and MySpace provide. Should your child choose to add you as a friend (a practice I actively promote), assume your access is merely probationary until you prove yourself to be a trustworthy parent who can hover at a safe distance. Commenting on your child's page, especially in the common areas, will send her friends fleeing and bring an abrupt end to your access. If you are genuinely concerned about the comments you read, consider an offline discussion. Bringing social concerns (online or off) to your child's attention in a private setting saves her from public embarrassment and ridicule.

"Erik added me as a friend when he started his Facebook account as a freshman in high school. I never abused the privilege by asking too many questions or prying into his social time. He always knew I was there, though, which made him more aware of what friends were posting on his page. It's been a win-win for me especially now that he is in college. I don't see him every day like I used to, but I still feel like I know what he is doing and what's important in his life."

—Lori, college mom, Santa Barbara, CA

Hiding in the shadows

Hovering too close or continually insisting in knowing your child's every move can quickly send him running for cover. Kids who want to keep their online identity and activity away from a parent's prying eyes have devised a formidable defense. In an effort to disguise their online activity, some kids create a dummy or "shadow" account that mirrors their real account in most areas. Typically, if a child creates two accounts the first will include her real name, a smattering of basic personal information, and a few candid photos of friends engaging in innocent acts of fun, intended to assure unknowing parents that all is well with their child's social life. The shadow account, often created under a false name, holds the answers to the child's true online activity. In rare cases, children engage in unlawful or flagrantly disrespectful behavior there. With the recent upsurge in monitoring of these types of accounts across the general population of users, suspicious behavior among minors has come under increased scrutiny. Users of any age who violate the terms of agreement can have their account privileges revoked without advance notice. It's not easy to coax a child out from the shadows and toward the beginning of a more trusting relationship. Take time to acknowledge the importance of your child's personal autonomy, and with time you may find your way back to a healthy relationship based on trust and honesty.

Given the massive amount of negative media attention given to social networking, it's easy to overlook the vast majority of positive interactions that a virtual connection with friends can provide. Despite the media message that there's a prevalence of online predators, in reality kids tend to avoid forming friendships with people online who fall too far outside their immediate group of friends in the offline world. Unlike most adult users, kids and teens use their social network to stay connected with a limited number of friends who are often confined to a small geographic location. School-based groups and citywide networks form the majority of connections among kids in the twelve-to-seventeen-year-old age group. In essence, kids take the friendships they have offline and continue them online. Adults, in contrast, use their network to stay connected with friends, family members, and business colleagues who span the globe. As adults we use the same technology but for a completely different type of communication and connection. Unfortunately, media attention focuses on the rare occasions when the worlds of adults and children collide.

I hope your journey through cyberspace helps you create a solid plan for your family's safe and equitable internet use. We'll now take a more detailed look at how families grow together (and apart) during the middle school years. In the final chapter, we will explore the importance of creating a vision for your family's ongoing growth and happiness that will help guide everyone through a traditionally troublesome time. The challenge to stay on course requires input from trusted friends, mentors, and coaches who will form the basis of your family's support team for years to come.

CHAPTER 6

Thriving as a Family during Middle School

"Coming together is a beginning. Keeping together is progress. Working together is success."   *—Henry Ford*

"The structure of families has changed from when I was a kid. My mom stayed at home and supervised our after-school time. If we went to a friend's house, she knew we would be supervised or we didn't go. Today in many families both parents work, and a lot of kids are left unsupervised to socialize with friends until the evening hours. I think a lot of parents just don't realize the critical role they play in their child's success. I didn't realize how important my role was until Zack brought home a paper he had written for his eighth grade English class. In the paper he talked about how he wished I hadn't given him so much space to try new things earlier in the middle school years. The independence he had fought so hard for now seemed to be a motivating factor for us both to make a change. If we were going to make it through the high school years, we needed to try something different."
                              —Maureen, high school mom, San Anselmo, CA

THE PREVIOUS CHAPTERS of this book have given you the foundation for guiding and supporting your child through many of middle school's most challenging aspects. In this final chapter we will look at how your parenting role will grow and change as you confront the *daily* challenges of adolescence. Although the ideas presented here are grounded in research and practice, be aware that simply reading them is not enough; they require consistent action.

We begin with a look at what adolescents wish parents knew. Drawn from my conversations with children and parents over the past twenty years, the following list highlights high-priority concerns that, if neglected, can quickly lead to frustration between family members. Read this list with careful and thorough consideration, keeping in mind that what kids perceive they need and want is often different from what will actually move them forward in their development. The list serves as a launching point for further discussion about vision, goals, and a solid foundation of emotional support for your child in the years ahead.

- My friends are really important to me right now. Help me see the importance of family while still finding time to spend with friends.
- Teach me how to make choices and accept consequences. Don't bail me out when accepting the consequences of my choices would help me learn important life lessons.
- I like my privacy at home. Help me learn how to earn your respect at home so that, in turn, I can feel respected.
- I like consistency even though I won't admit it. Too much freedom without consequences will lead me to trouble.
- I appreciate having a list of things to do and a deadline for completing them. Continued nagging or a never-ending list of tasks bugs me.
- Please don't choose my extracurricular activities for me or push me to participate in an activity when it's obvious I'm not interested.
- Let's try to avoid arguing about school. If you expect me to get A's and B's in school then say so. Telling me to "Give my best effort" doesn't give me a clear picture of the grades you expect to see on my report card.
- When I am feeling down, give me some time and space to sort out my emotions. Let me know that you will be ready to listen when I am ready to talk.

- I am beginning to notice my appearance more than I did in the past. Please don't comment on how I look, especially in public or around my friends—it's embarrassing.

This list identifies concerns and challenges expressed by most adolescents; you will find that your child's needs are unique and continually changing. Learning to appreciate your child's changing perspective while maintaining your own is an ongoing challenge, but one worth exploring.

Unofficial Adolescent Credo

In talking with parents about the middle school years, I've developed a useful resource I call the Unofficial Adolescent Credo. Understanding these basic underpinnings of the adolescent mind-set can help to alleviate misunderstandings between adults and kids.

I need your help even though I rarely ask. Unsolicited assistance is rarely appreciated, particularly when friends are around. Finding ways to remain present, yet invisible, takes time and practice. Look for opportunities when you can spend time alone with your child. A car ride to pick up friends or the rare moment at home without the rest of the family offer opportune moments for your child to ask for your guidance. But the car ride to and from school typically is less ideal. A day at school requires incredible focus for most kids, and the minutes before and after school can be filled with emotion, so don't count on these times for meaningful interactions. Although your child may ask for your help less often than in the past, know that when he does ask, your words and subsequent actions will have incredible impact.

Ask me to participate in meaningful ways. I may not accept your invitations; but I do appreciate your effort to include me. Even though taking out the trash or doing light housework may be a part of what you expect from your child, completing chores doesn't qualify as meaningful participation. Adolescents are looking for situations that would benefit from their input. Planning the week's meals or negotiating rides for after-school events could be wonderful opportunities for your child to participate in or even take charge of the planning process. When parents include their kids in family decision making, everybody wins. Kids feel appreciated and acknowledged. Parents benefit by watching their children grow into independent problem-solvers.

I'm moody at times. I may be having a bad day and just need some time to cool off. It takes a shift in your parental mind-set to not jump in and try to make everything all right. The natural instinct for most parents is to play the problem-solver role. But confronting an upset adolescent at the wrong time can quickly lead to a full-scale verbal assault—and leave you feeling sad and frustrated. When you sense that your child is heading for a blowup (or meltdown), find a safe place to wait until the wave of emotion passes you by. When the waters seem calm again, offer your support by asking "Is there anything you want to talk about?" With time and patience you will learn how and when to offer support. Remember, parenting is an ongoing learning process.

Your continued caring tells me you still want me around even when I'm difficult. Second only to the teen years, a child's transition to adolescence can leave parents nearly speechless at times. Seemingly illogical demands followed by relentless pleas bring even the most patient parents to a place of disbelief. "Where did my child go?" is a familiar question shared among middle school parents. The key to defusing these discussions is to leave before either one of you says something that will be regretted later. When you sense your emotions heating up, walk away. As you leave, acknowledge that you expect to return in a few minutes with a question or statement that will move the discussion away from the negative and toward the productive.

"My mom really hung in there with me this year. There were times when I was moody and didn't have many nice things to say. She kept telling me she would be there when I wanted to talk. Knowing that she cared about me made a big difference in my life."

—Melanie, seventh grader, New York, NY

Needs are different than wants

At times, an adolescent's list of wants may seem insatiable. Shifting the focus from giving a child what he wants to providing what he needs may help to reduce the frustration many parents feel on an ongoing basis. When a child says, "I want a new Xbox" or "Everyone else has one, why can't I?" he's expressing what he wants. Expressing a want is often a substitute for trying to satisfy a need that has gone unmet. You'll learn over time that simply giving him whatever he says he wants doesn't seem to truly satisfy him. If instead you consistently meet his *needs* (such as giving him your full attention or setting sensible limits on outside socializing so he feels safe and knows you care), you can expect to see evidence of real satisfaction in your child—including higher levels of self-esteem as well as increased achievement in school.

Families need support

Statistics from the United States Census Bureau show the average population per household has dwindled from nearly 5 people in the early 1900s to a mere 2.5 people as of the recent 2006 census recording. This trend has led to a fundamental shift in the structure of American families, from larger extended families and close-knit neighborhoods to smaller nuclear families, single-family homes, and loosely connected communities. In addition, kids these days rarely engage in activities with neighborhood friends (with neighboring parents close by or even involved), choosing instead to participate in cross-town activities. Increasingly, kids will travel thirty minutes to the swim club or the arts center for music lessons instead of shooting hoops in the driveway.

Smaller families plus less time spent together equals less support for children at a time when they need greater support. You can meet this growing need by creating a *support team*. Not unlike a sports team, a family's support team consists of people outside your nuclear family who fill specific roles and are brought together for a singular purpose. Your support team must function to ensure the future success of your child and family. You'll build and solidify the roster of players over time. Some players resign their positions, making room for new, more productive members to join the squad.

The fall season is fast approaching. Begin building your team today, using the following ideas as a guide.

Building your support team

According to the U.S. Census Bureau, today's generation of school-age children spend the majority of their waking hours in the care of someone other than their parents. Given the influence that teachers, coaches, mentors, and extended family members have on a child's development, it's essential to build a relationship with this group of people. You'll need to make a shift in your usual parental role to create a team of focused and motivated individuals who will continually support the ongoing growth of your child.

To gain the extended support that families had naturally a generation or two ago, you need to assemble a roster of supportive team players that extends beyond the walls of your family home. Building the foundation of that strong support team begins at home. With a clear vision in place and a set of realistic goals to pursue, you are ready to add more members to your team.

Create a roster. Who will affect your child's life this year? Think of the word *team* as meant to include anyone who has the ability to Teach, Encourage, Advocate for, or Motivate your child on a weekly basis, then begin by listing people who fit this description. Most middle schoolers will have a minimum of five teachers who will play a critical role in their lives. Their influence in the hour they spend with your child every weekday can have a tremendous impact on your child's ability to grow both academically and socially. Outside of the classroom, schools have a full-time staff of counselors and administrators who can also fill spots on your roster. Principals and student counselors can turn potentially sticky situations into positive ones in the course of a single conversation. Connecting with these folks is crucial to building a solid team roster. Off campus, look for coaches and mentors who you believe will support the same morals and values that you hope to impart to your child. Their participation in the after-school hours rounds out the day for your child and can often set the tone for the evening hours at home. Family friends and extended family members could be possible additions as well. Keep the door open for anyone who fits the description of a potential TEAM member.

Position the players. With a completed team roster, identify when and where your child will see these critical people. Teachers and school personnel typically fall within a specified seven-hour time block on a regular Monday-through-Friday schedule. However, the after-school hours are equally important, so be sure you include on the support team whoever will supervise your child beyond the conclusion of the school day. Now you've created an accurate picture of your child's life and the role that each adult will play this year.

Connect. The beginning of a school year marks the start of many new relationships. During the first few weeks of school, take a few minutes to communicate with each person on your roster. Send a written note or email, or share a quick conversation in person. The message to convey is short and sincere: "Hi, I just wanted you to know how excited I am to have you in my child's life this year." This quick introduction sends a powerful message to everyone on your team about the importance of their role for your family. Connecting with each team member puts the players into action.

When presented with an opportunity to become part of a support team, most people are ready and willing to offer their assistance in any way possible.

Check in. Make an ongoing effort to maintain those team relationships over time. You can't just send an email in the opening weeks of the school year and then fail to connect in the following months. And don't wait until a problem arises to initiate a conversation. Every two to three weeks, check in with each of the people on your roster. Begin with an open-ended question; this allows the conversation about your child to evolve naturally. If instead you use a leading question—like "How was her behavior today?" or "Were there any problems?"—you're narrowing the focus to a potentially negative set of comments that may create greater distance between you and the key adults in your child's life, and you may lose the opportunity to share positive comments or questions.

Sustaining the team takes ongoing communication in the form of acknowledgments and praise. A short voicemail that expresses your heartfelt thanks for a coach's extra time and commitment to your child's progress does wonders for solidifying a relationship.

Celebrate. Reaching milestones and achieving goals are cause for celebration. Place a quick call to your child's teacher after the conclusion of a class play or project. Express your acknowledgment and appreciation—two characteristics of supportive teams. The more often team members celebrate together, the stronger the relationship grows.

Remember, for a relationship to grow, it requires both parties to give. The time you spend acknowledging and praising the people on your team is an investment that grows over time. Acknowledge the simple things that people do for your child. No deed is too small or insignificant. As a former teacher, I well remember how I relished receiving notes from parents (and kids) in which they expressed their joy in being part of the classroom. Teachers in particular love to receive these simple kudos. Although they show up and give it their all without intending to receive a reward, they truly appreciate the sentiments of parents who take the time to notice their efforts. The same can be said for any of the members on your team. Look for ways to stay connected with the people who are closest to your child and family. These folks are the ones who will come through for you if you need a shoulder to lean on.

Meaningful participation

Most adolescents, if asked, wouldn't admit their desire to actively engage in family activities, but when they do take part in the planning, the result is usually positive. Decisions about family vacations or weekly dinner plans give your child real opportunities to contribute to the ongoing growth of your family. Be on the lookout for regular, substantive issues that warrant your child's contribution; this will help to fulfill his need for meaningful participation.

Too often, we parents let an overwhelming feeling of responsibility for creating the ideal childhood get in the way of simply enjoying our time together with our kids, in the moment. If your parenting mind can't let go of its need to control, plan, and closely scrutinize every detail, you'll leave no room for the serendipity that a young adolescent mind might bring to the table. Parents who like this role of organizer and master planner have particular trouble relinquishing the position. Assuming a new role requires a steady diet of shared decision making. By bringing your family together at regular intervals through a strategy called the weekly check-in, you can ease the transition in your parenting role as well as relieve some of the stress that comes from assuming sole responsibility for all matters that affect your family.

"It meant a lot to me when my parents asked for my ideas about where we should go on our next family vacation. I felt like they were treating me like someone who mattered."

—*Jake, seventh grader, Las Vegas, NV*

Family meetings don't work

Does the term *family meeting* bring back fond memories from your childhood? No? Many of my experiences as both a child and now as an adult talking with children have confirmed that family meetings follow a typical pattern: parents speak, children listen. Reflecting on my own childhood experiences, I remember my parents focusing on their expectations of responsibility and respect. As their accusations and my defenses escalated, most meetings took on an adversarial tone. Not exactly a picture-perfect moment of quality family time together. You can provide a different experience by reframing the family meeting as a "weekly check-in." Different from the traditional family meeting, the weekly check-in focuses on positive comments, goal setting, and acknowledgment of effort and achievement. The notion behind the check-in is simply to bring everyone together as the name implies—to check in. Rather than waiting for problems to arise that would dictate a call to action, you hold check-ins regularly; this helps stave off potential trouble before it reaches a critical reactionary state.

Finding the time to schedule a weekly check-in is probably the greatest obstacle to overcome. Look for a time, preferably on a Sunday or Monday before you get too far into the week, when your entire family can share twenty to thirty minutes of uninterrupted time.

Steps to productive check-ins

Begin with appreciations. Set the tone for a positive discussion by giving everyone the opportunity to share an appreciation with someone else in the family. "Thank you for taking me to the movies" or "I appreciate your helping with dinner" are examples of simple yet powerful appreciations.

Acknowledge effort. Next, turn your family's focus to acknowledging effort and its connection to achievement. It's easy for a child to say, "I'm so busy with homework, studying, and after-school activities. You don't understand, Mom." When parents share examples from their lives that highlight their own efforts, kids begin to realize that effort and perseverance are issues that all family members struggle with. By sharing authentic experiences, you create a team mentality in your adolescent's developing mind. Your child won't be so quick to complain about the homework load when she realizes that you too are struggling to muster the effort to deal with life's daily challenges. Give everyone at the table a few minutes to talk about the effort they have given throughout the week; this restores team camaraderie and naturally leads into the goal-setting portion of your check-in.

Plan for the future. Goal setting keeps people moving forward. Goals need not be long, drawn-out lifelong pursuits. In fact, short-term goals function better when it comes to the weekly check-in. Creating a goal that can be achieved during a seven-day period confines effort and focus to a workable time frame for everyone. Goals can focus on personal pursuits, like a commitment to exercising three times during the coming week, or academic achievements, for which the goal might be to study every evening in preparation for the big test on Friday. In either case, the stated goal should focus on the effort required to achieve the goal and not merely the product you aim to achieve. Getting straight A's on the quarterly report card is not achievable within a seven-day period; making an outstanding effort in preparation for the weekly math test is both achievable and directly connected to the effort a child chooses to expend.

Check the calendar. Small enough to fit on a desk, yet large enough to display a month of activities at a glance, a desktop calendar should be standard equipment for any adolescent making the transition to middle school. Keep the calendar in a location that's equally accessible for all family members, and begin to note events or commitments that will occur in the coming week. Charting the week's events gives everyone a snapshot of the family's activity load for the coming week as well as an anticipatory look at any potential conflicts. Now you all can troubleshoot time conflicts and double bookings as a family activity rather than something Mom and Dad have to solve. An evening commitment at work could easily conflict with a late-afternoon baseball practice. This conflict presents a good opportunity for your child to step in and offer a possible solution. Look for these exercises in conflict resolution as times of growth for your family. As a parent you have the chance to step aside and share responsibility with your child, who wants to contribute. These win-win situations don't come along too often, so take advantage of the ones that do come your way by hearing and acknowledging your child's voice.

"Although high school has its own challenges, Max and I have a relationship now that allows us to face those challenges together. We still have arguments, but now we work together to make choices that affect his future. We have a mutual respect for each other that has grown out of finding time to talk about what he wants to achieve and how I can best support him."

—Melanie, high school parent, Thousand Oaks, CA

Schedule the next check-in. Before everyone heads out to start the week, take a final moment to plot a date during the following week when you will come back together for your next check-in. In twenty-five minutes your family will have had the opportunity to appreciate each other, focus on acknowledging effort, plan for the future, and problem-solve your way to a more connected school year.

Picture, plan, and promote time together

Family dinners with everyone gathered around plates of home-made food are heartwarming to think about, but these Norman Rockwell renditions of the American family are far from what most of us experience on a daily basis. For many families, including ours, mealtimes may not be the ideal times to bring everyone together. Although we strive to share at least one meal together each day, there are days when we are moving in too many different directions. The alternative for many families is finding time outside of traditional chow time to connect and share valuable experiences together. Try each of the following strategies to identify some of the places where your family might find time to share. My guess is that you will discover more opportunities than you previously thought existed.

Soliciting participation and support for the home team takes time and ongoing effort. The "picture, plan, and promote" strategy can be a powerful way to bring family members together in a way that benefits everyone.

Picture. Take five minutes to recall the events that have brought your family together in meaningful ways. Sharing a meal, enjoying a movie, and taking family trips garner the top spots on many lists.

Plan. Find the family calendar and look for opportunities to designate as family time. Plotting a date on the calendar increases the possibility of going to the beach, sharing a picnic, or taking a weekend excursion tenfold.

Promote. If spending time together as a family has not been a regular part of the weekly routine, there may be some apprehension or, in some cases, strong opposition to planned family gatherings. By including everyone in the planning process, family time becomes a group effort in which everyone has something invested.

"In the Moran family, everyone is responsible for preparing one part
of the weekly family dinner. Our six-year-old likes making ice cream
sundaes, so dessert is usually his contribution. Julie, our thirteen-
year-old, typically opts for an original creation of vegetables or fruit.
Sharing dinner together as a family keeps us talking and working
together."   —Dee Moran, mother of two, Scottsdale, AZ

Using the "picture, plan, and promote" strategy creates an initial boost of energy and motivation among family members that
can launch the home team forward in September. But it can be
more difficult to maintain excitement over the long haul.

It takes ongoing effort to sustain momentum through consistent
communication among family members. The weekly check-in is a
great routine to begin at the start of the school year. When families
become accustomed to regular and frequent communication, they
can move beyond the scheduled approach that a weekly check-in
promotes. Varying the venue also helps families come together.
Search for new and engaging activities and environments for your
family to explore this year that will bring new life to family gatherings and, above all, keep fun at the heart of your interactions.

Chart a strategy

If you like more structure and appreciate the appeal of a formal
calendar of events, then you may find the charting strategy more
useful. The goal of this activity is to predict when family members
will come together so that the time you share is more meaningful. Anticipating moments of shared time gives you a wonderful
opportunity to focus on the interactions you want to have rather
than waiting for those moments to arrive and then reacting to
whatever shows up.

On a standard sheet of lined paper, create a chart with four
columns. From left to right, label the columns Daily, Weekly,
Quarterly, and Annually.

Fill the chart with events or activities that will involve the whole family. Begin with the Daily and Weekly columns, then move across the page as ideas come to mind. After you have exhausted the list of activities that involve everyone, turn to activities that only a few family members might take part in (a trip to the movie theater or a lunch together could provide the ideal setting for you and your child to connect, separate from the whole family). Sharing special time with a child or spouse can be just as important to keeping the family together as a whole-family experience.

Consider planning a mini-vacation or long weekend once a quarter. These two-to-three-day excursions can be as basic as a trip to your local camping area or a short visit to see extended family members. In the "Annually" column include birthdays—both those of your immediate family and any other birthdays that your family celebrates with either close friends or extended family members. Holidays belong in this column. Are you planning to stay at home or travel for any of the major holidays on your calendar? Anticipating these extended family times can help you start coordinating a few planned activities that will bring everyone together. Finally, add an extended trip to the list of annual family events, if possible. As with the mini-vacations, don't feel compelled to plan a grand, multi-week adventure that leaves your bank account depleted for months. The goal in planning your trip is to create a time that brings everyone together to share and appreciate each other.

Staying connected throughout the middle school years contributes significantly to your child's growth as a productive and healthy adolescent. Regular conversations with you and the members of your support team create a web of security that children need in order to feel comfortable as they take risks and explore the world.

Why expectations are important

It is important for middle school parents to create and communicate a set of high expectations for your child's ongoing development. But be careful not to confuse high expectations with unrealistic goals that have little to no hope of being realized. High expectations clearly articulate the boundaries that you believe to be achievable in your child's life. The challenge comes in trying to accurately and objectively determine what is appropriate for your child, given his current level of development. In the area of academic achievement, parents can easily overload their child with advanced classes and optional electives that push the child beyond the limit of what's possible. What a parent believes to be realistic and what an adolescent perceives as realistic can differ dramatically. The following story helps to illustrate this point.

Having become accustomed to daughter Carey's steady progress of A's and B's in elementary school, her parents registered her for the honors courses in middle school. Their unstated expectation was that Carey's level of achievement would remain on par with her past performance. After the first few weeks of school, Carey found herself overwhelmed with assignments and anxiety over learning the course content. The B's and C's on Carey's first report card reflected her quarter-long struggle to achieve. Even though her effort had remained high, the rigor of the coursework had increased. The argument that followed ended with an ultimatum from Carey's parents: "Things had better change, or else."

Although the elementary school years create the foundation for a child's achievement, parents should be careful when scheduling classes for the first middle school year. Typically the workload of upper elementary school courses won't compare to a full slate of classes at the middle school level. Before you schedule fall classes, have a conversation with your child about the challenges that lie ahead. It's part of your coaching role to encourage your child to take a path that will stretch his ability to learn and grow. As the discussion unfolds, don't forget to ask your child, "What do you think? Does this list of classes sound too challenging?" rather than making the assumption that you and you alone know what's best. Over the preceding six to seven years of school your child has also developed an acute sense of what "challenging" looks like with respect to instruction and assignments. Co-creating the year's class schedule brings two added benefits. First, your child will appreciate being included in decisions that affect his life. Second, by sharing responsibility for course planning you forge a stronger bond with your child that will get you through some of the difficult times that lie ahead.

If Carey and her parents had taken a few moments to create a clear set of expectations, they might have avoided an argument later. Admittedly, it's tough to determine an appropriate level of challenge that will stretch a child without subsequently diminishing her zeal for exploring the unknown—but you'll find it well worth the effort.

Creating goals and a path for growth

Creating goals takes practice. We are not born with the innate ability to create a direct path toward achievement. Goal setting challenges us to focus on what we really want and then plot a path that will eventually lead us there. It's a rare child who can clearly state what she wants to achieve when it comes to the grades on her report card. The right answer seems to be, "All A's." But when asked, most adolescents admit that getting straight A's is what their *parents* want to hear. The reality of what shows up on the report card may be dramatically different. So how do parents and kids come together to talk about what's realistic while still promoting a healthy level of challenge?

The first step may be to talk about areas of challenge. Does your child's class schedule present a grim picture of endless homework? Perhaps the sheer number of classes seems like an overwhelming responsibility. What about the after-school schedule of activities? Will the three-days-a-week practice schedule leave time for a full night of homework as well as time to talk with friends? Without the prior experience of managing multiple schedules and expectations, kids can become anxious about the host of potential unknowns. It's vital that you help your child accurately gauge where and when challenges will occur. Begin by creating a list that focuses on two to three areas of challenge for the coming year. Ask your child for her ideas as you co-create the list. Common items for this list are having the time to finish all homework, spending time with friends, getting enough sleep, staying healthy, and fulfilling extracurricular responsibilities.

With a clearer picture of the difficulties in mind, turn your discussion to past achievements and challenges. The elementary school years provide a good primer for what lies ahead. Even though your child may not have had the challenge of managing multiple teacher expectations, she undoubtedly studied a host of different topics that required a significant amount of homework. Do you recall how much homework time the average night included? Tracking homework hours during the elementary years will provide you and your child with a clearer idea of what to expect when the middle school homework begins to arrive. Middle school classes each typically average a minimum of thirty minutes a night of homework. A quick calculation tells you that the typical seven period schedule could easily result in three and a half hours of work each evening! Would a jump in homework time push your child past the point of being able to focus and create quality assignments? If so, you should take the opportunity to share your thoughts about the preceding years and guide your child to reduce his course load to a level that may be more in tune with his current ability. It can be difficult for a child of middle school age to find the right balance between taking on too much and near boredom.

Creating a manageable academic schedule is one slice, albeit a significant one, of a middle schooler's life. Extracurricular schedules and socializing with friends also account for a fair amount of time each week. Most kids at this age have difficulty learning how to manage multiple schedules and responsibilities. Throughout elementary school you may have taken responsibility for managing your child's schedule. The transition to middle school, though, begins a new era. Your child and most of the other adults in his life will want to shift the responsibility out of your hands. As an intermediate step to giving up complete control, consider donning a coaching hat, and with it a slightly different role.

As a coach you still assume great responsibility for teaching your child. Completing homework, managing time, and maintaining friendships all require ongoing education that you can provide. In a coaching role, however, you hand over responsibility to your child when it comes time to put his new skills into action. Guiding your child through the goal-setting process is a wonderful way to step into your new coaching role.

By creating a realistic set of goals that focus on action-oriented objectives, you and your child can bring balance to his schedule as well as his emotional state. A child who is accustomed to focusing in short bursts of time may well struggle with looking forward toward potential goals. Start small, with goals that can be achieved in a short time period (one to two days). Your role as a coach can be integral in helping your child create and achieve a realistic set of goals leading to long-term success during the middle school years.

Action-oriented versus outcome-based goals

The achievement of *action-oriented* goals depends entirely on the effort of the person trying to achieve the goals. The achievement of *outcome-based* goals often depends on a host of variables, many of which are not under the direct control of the goal seeker. In the case of the outcome-based goal in the pair of examples that follow, the math teacher ultimately decides which questions appear on tests, the project requirements, and the value of nightly homework assignments, all of which determine a student's final grade.

Action-oriented goal: I want to improve my current grade in math.

Outcome-based goal: I want an A in math.

With a focus on keeping effort at the core of the goals your child creates, try the following seven-day goal-setting strategy.

Step One: Work with your middle schooler to create an action-oriented goal that can be achieved in the next seven days. Record it on a piece of paper with the title, "My goal for the next seven days." A seven-day period is short enough for adolescents to visualize and allows them enough time to demonstrate progress through specific actions. One example of an action-oriented goal is, "I want to improve my test grades." But working with your child means that you ask questions and wait for answers—not the other way around.

Step Two: Ask your middle schooler, "What is one thing you can do today that would help you to achieve your goal?" and have her record the answer on the goal-setting paper. With their focus on *today*, most adolescents immediately move into an action mind-set: "If I can do one thing today, I am one step closer to achieving my goal." Put one foot in front of the other—forward movement creates momentum.

Step Three: Follow up the previous question by asking, "What can you do tomorrow that would help you to achieve your goal?" As in the preceding steps, continue to add responses to the goal-setting paper. Focusing on tomorrow gives your child the opportunity to think about the future. Although tomorrow doesn't seem far away to most adults, many teens don't have a clue about what is going to happen in the next twenty-four hours. Thinking about what's next (like completing the test study guide) automatically gives the brain a focus point. When a seed has been planted, the adolescent brain naturally begins to take action to nurture the seed's growth. Translation: *your middle schooler's brain will take action even if his physical body does not.* Keep this strategy in mind for other ideas you would like your middle schooler to consider.

Step Four: Depending on your middle schooler's state of mind and attitude after articulating his responses to the first three steps, you might decide to forgo this step. If your conversation is still relatively civil, then proceed with the following question: "What can you do over the next seven days [target the exact day—seven days from now could easily seem like seven weeks from now in an adolescent's mind] that will help you to achieve your goal?" Add any new ideas to the goal-setting paper. The purpose of looking seven days into the future is to use the momentum your adolescent has generated in the first two days to propel him forward toward the successful achievement of his goal.

Step Five: Celebrate achievement. On day seven, ask your child two questions: "What did you do this week to achieve your goal?" and "How can we celebrate?" Yes, you can make the assumption that your child's goal was achieved. When you anticipate achievement, remarkable things happen. Your celebration doesn't have to be anything elaborate—just something he will enjoy.

Through small, consistent achievements, adolescents learn how to develop a healthy sense of independence. Imagine your sense of pride when your child leaves home years from now with the confidence and ability to succeed on his own.

Although academic achievement can easily become the focus of parental concern, your adolescent also needs a clear and consistent set of expectations for his role as a member of your family. Arguments frequently erupt over issues of curfew, computer time, phone calls, and a host of other peer-related issues. To maintain a sane environment in your home and among the members of your family, you'll need to develop a clear set of expectations for each of the trouble spots. As you consider your stance on the issues just listed, think about the consequences you are willing to enforce should your child fail to live up to the expectations you have shared with him. Consistency in enforcing consequences is just as important as the actual expectations you choose to implement at home. Even though most adolescents wouldn't admit to it in the moment, they want consistency; in fact, they thrive on it—particularly when it comes from their parents.

"I wish my mom hadn't given me so much space to try new things in junior high. I wouldn't have liked hearing it, but I wouldn't have gotten into so much trouble." —Jackson, eighth grader, Seattle, WA

"The elementary school years were tough, especially his last year. Chad was missing homework assignments and scoring low on tests and projects. This year was a lot different. I talked to him before the school started. We established a set of expectations for his schoolwork." —Jamie, middle school mom, San Diego, CA

With a clearer picture of how to identify and meet your child's needs, let's take the next step toward builder a stronger and more productive family. This begins with creating a vision of what you would like your family to be.

The connection between vision and goals

If creating a vision is your blueprint for success, then goal setting and achievement are the building blocks you'll use to assemble it. Goals are the specific actions or outcomes that bring you closer to realizing your vision.

"In school you have report cards to report your progress; in the workplace, there are many different measures of success. For both parents and adolescents, some of the most defining moments are the most basic ones. When you receive an unsolicited compliment about your child from another adult or parent—that is a defining moment. You

can be challenged on the home front with your teenager, yet find out
this same defiant teenager did something to stand out in a positive way.
In my opinion, that's one of the greatest rewards a parent can receive."
—Denise, parent of two, Agoura Hills, CA

Envision the ideal school year

Is academic achievement at the top of the list, or do you hope this
will be the year your child breaks out of her social shell? Who
will guide your child's development? A vision defines a direction
toward a goal. Realizing a vision requires support from a motivated
group of individuals—a team of people who band together through
adversity, inspire motivation, and acknowledge achievement.

Take ten minutes to create a list of adjectives that describes how
you envision your family in the coming year. The adjectives on
your list are the foundation of your vision for the coming middle
school year. Next, create a series of statements that connect the
adjectives on your list with specific actions that you believe will
bring your vision to life.

For example, one of your goals may be for the family to be less
stressed and more relaxed. Short day trips or mini-vacations can
help everyone take a break from the usual routine; often resulting
in renewed appreciation of staying connected. Relaxed families
often benefit from time to do what they enjoy most. Sometimes
this means giving each member the chance to engage in an activity separately. The time you each spend alone may help bring a
more relaxed feeling to the time you share together.

Define year-long goals

Successful families work together as a team to create both short-
and long-term objectives. Perhaps the time has come for a strategic
planning session with your family. Check your calendar and select
a time when the family can spend an hour together. Congratulations! With a date on the calendar you have taken the first step
toward committing to action.

When the time comes, open your meeting with the following question: "If our year went exactly the way we wish it would, what would we have achieved by June?" Each person should have the opportunity to respond and share ideas without interruption or debate. Record the responses on a piece of paper. Some goals may focus on academic achievement; others may have a more personal focus. The more specific and measurable these outcomes are, the easier it will be for each member of your family to follow through toward completion of his or her goals. For example, your child's goals may look like this: "Join the club soccer team" and "Earn a B average in school."

Accept all ideas without judgment. When all have added their ideas, take a moment to review the list by reading each idea aloud. Allow time for any needed adjustments. Resist the temptation to edit your child's ideas. Adolescents place great value on their ability to share ideas in a meaningful way. Making changes to what your child has said removes any authenticity or meaning from the activity and puts the decision-making power back into your hands. You can ask your child to commit to achieving a series of goals only if you freely give him the power to decide what those goals are.

Written goals act like magnets, pulling the creators toward the manifestation of their dreams. Yet many families forgo this very important exercise, opting instead for a day-to-day approach to their year that may leave everyone frustrated and anxious. Written goals become measurable benchmarks for progress and thus are more powerful. Regularly reviewing your list of goals is like sailing with GPS navigation. If your boat veers off course, a quick glance helps you regain your bearings and progress toward your destination.

It takes time to define a series of goals. The real work is making a daily commitment to taking action that leads to the achievement of your goals. Many great plans fail mainly because people don't make the effort required to put the plan into action. One of the best ways to ensure that family members reach their goals is through ongoing communication that acknowledges achievement and celebrates success. Research shows that regular communication helps families stay connected during the adolescent years.

School, sports, and a variety of other extracurricular interests challenge a family's ability to stay connected during the school year. Before the back-to-school routine begins to take hold, think about how you would like your family to be this year. How often do all of you come together to share a meal, enjoy a weekend afternoon, or have a conversation? With a clear picture of how you would like your family to be, the path to realizing this ideal becomes clearer too.

Anticipate rough spots

Even the most well-devised plan will hit a few snags along the way. Anticipating the inevitable rough spots won't entirely eliminate frustrating moments or arguments, but it will help to minimize the intensity and frequency of challenging situations. What portion of the weekend will your child's budding social life consume? Does your family designate a specific portion of the weekend for together time? Attempt to strike a balance by sharing your plans for the impending weekend by midweek, while asking your child to do the same. Last minute invitations are inevitable for both kids and parents, but your response doesn't need to be. If accepting a spur-of-the-moment invite puts everyone's schedule in a bind or compromises a previously scheduled family event, consider turning down the invitation in favor of holding to your original plan.

In addition to the frustration associated with tightly scheduled weekends, families can fall prey to periodic angst connected with open periods of time when the regular routine disappears. Holidays and the long summer break from school are two typically tense times for families.

The break from school means a break from routine. Kids enjoy the extra leisure time, while parents busily prepare for the holiday festivities. Many of us feel compelled to participate in everything that comes our way, automatically accepting invitations for holiday parties, parades, and gift exchanges that we later regret. The added number of activities can result in extra stress during a time when there may already be an overload of regular commitments. Before the clamor and chaos of the holiday season set in, take a moment to sit back and envision your ideal holiday experience. Can fun and family coexist during the holidays? Where does holiday shopping and entertainment fit into your vision for the coming months? With a clear vision in place of how you want your holiday season to be, you have a much better chance of realizing your vision.

Long before the holiday season approaches, plan for a portion of your weekly check-in to include a family brainstorming session focused on the impending season of joy. Use the following activity to guide your brainstorming session. Commit to taking action on your ideas in the week that follows your initial vision planning session. Don't let yourself fall into the trap of thinking *The holidays are months away. I have more pressing things to do.* Plan ahead for what you want to experience, then delight in what actually unfolds.

Create the ideal holiday vision

Begin by creating a list of adjectives that describe your previous holiday experiences. Cross out any adjectives that don't create a positive picture in your mind. You may decide to throw out the entire list.

On a second piece of paper, list the adjectives that describe your ideal holiday season. Remember, this is your ideal so use words that truly represent the vision of what you want to experience. *Nice* and *good* don't create a vivid enough picture. If nice and good really mean *relaxed* and *peaceful*, then choose these more evocative words. The richer the description, the more likely you are to choose a course of action that matches it.

With the second list in hand, create one action statement for the coming day or days. The statement should define a specific action you and your family members can complete within the holiday that will bring you closer to realizing the ideal you have envisioned. If one of the adjectives on your list was *relaxed* you could use the following action statement, "I will find thirty minutes in the coming week to engage in an activity I enjoy." Commit yourself to this activity by circling a date on the calendar.

Continue to create action statements every several days that drive you toward your ideal vision for the holidays. With a frequent and consistent commitment to your family's vision, your set of action statements will naturally begin to bring you closer to realizing your ideal. Revisit your list of adjectives every week. Add new words to the list at any time as long as they align with your original vision.

When opportunities arise to engage in holiday activities, consider whether your involvement would bring you closer to or further from your ideal. With a clear picture in mind, it will be easier to decide to pass on certain activities.

Plan for a productive and engaging summer

Do you know how some kids look forward to summer? From around the start of Daylight Saving Time, kids begin living for the time when school is out. Parents, in comparison, often dread the freedom summer brings; they view the three-month stretch as an ongoing challenge of keeping their kids busy and out of trouble.

With the plethora of opportunities summer offers, parents need to narrow the field and eliminate those activities that don't fit with their child's interests. Here are three ways parents can help their children identify potential interests.

Direction. From your child's activities in elementary school, some lines of interest should already be apparent. Are they interested in travel, music, mathematics, art, or computers? One of the easiest ways to uncover hidden interests is for parents and kids to visit a bookstore three to five times over the next few weeks and buy a couple of magazines on each visit. The only caveat is that you choose different magazines each time.

On the first few visits, kids tend to focus on similar magazines. Your child may get frustrated when forced to choose a magazine covering a new interest. But over time (and probably without ever letting anyone know) kids actually begin to appreciate the challenge of seeking out new interests. Without the continued opportunity for discovery, kids return to the tried-and-true set of interests and activities, much like the magazine subscription whose issues continue to arrive but no one ever reads any more.

Gifts. What pursuits come naturally to your child? Children are gifted in many areas—some physically, others mentally, others musically or emotionally, still others intuitively. It seems that by age thirteen, many children begin to show their personalities, and their gifts shine through. The trick to effectively recognizing and acknowledging children's assets is to show them real-life examples of how their particular gifts are rewarded.

Motivation. Many parents are concerned and interested to find some area that interests their child, and they spend a lot of time and resources in search of motivation. There are many easy ways to introduce the motivating factors that children and their families need in order to experience fulfillment and success. The basic idea is, celebrate every success! Each time your child succeeds, make a big deal about it. Put a call in to the grandparents. Brag about it to your friends. Put up a sign by the dinner table. Yes, your child will roll her eyes and call you crazy, but secretly she'll feel outstanding simply because you are noticing her.

Another tactic to approaching the summer months requires more scheduling on the parent end. Kids have spent the past nine months of the school year researching, studying, and completing homework assignments. Now it's your turn. Pull out a calendar, preferably one that shows the entire month at a glance. Begin by filling in the events and activities you have already scheduled. Include everything from vacations to sports competitions. How much time is left to plan for?

Take five minutes to create a list of activities you think your child would enjoy. Do you notice any patterns in the activities you listed? Does your child enjoy the outdoors rather than indoor activities? Has volunteering time in the community been an interest? Does he seem to prefer individual activities or group settings?

Armed with a better sense of who your child is and the types of activities he prefers, you can more efficiently filter out opportunities that don't fit his interests. Your goal at this stage of the planning process is to create a list of ten to twelve ideas to share with your child. Start with the newspaper or your city's summer activity guide, adding activities to your list that might be of interest to your child. Next consider the wide range of volunteer and internship opportunities. Are there businesses within walking distance from your home that might need occasional assistance? Drop by and talk with a few business owners to inquire about their need for occasional volunteer assistance or a summer internship.

Beyond volunteering, consider contacting your local community service organization or church about day trips or weekend expeditions to nearby destinations. Typically, adults who enjoy mentoring kids staff these short treks. Look for a staff-to-child ratio of 1:10 or better. Even the most qualified staff can be challenged when the number of kids becomes too great. Consider adding mentoring opportunities to your research agenda. Most cities have a Big Brother/Big Sister program connecting teens and younger children in structured mentoring activities. Generally, kids rise to the occasion when asked to provide guidance for younger children.

Continue adding to your list as you find new and potentially engaging opportunities. Put a date on the calendar, preferably in early May, to talk with your child about planning for the summer months. The sooner you plan this meeting, the more time you both have to seek out activities and plan for a productive and engaging summer.

For some parents, scheduling activities is not the challenge. Finding time to recoup and relax before returning the school years proves to be the real challenge. Kids today are busier than ever. Many cities have large-scale programs that keep students busy from dawn till dusk (and often later). It's important to strike the right balance between being too busy and and being so idle it's boring. Here are some ways you can sustain engagement while finding time for a healthy amount of rest and relaxation.

By creating a "summer growth plan" (don't worry, it sounds much more formal than it really is), it will be easier to identify activities that spark interest and the ones you want to steer clear of. Having established a weekly check-in routine, you can use it to begin talking with your kids about summer opportunities. The summer vacation discussion gives the family an opportunity to share what kinds of things are current. What timing constraints do you have? For example, is the family taking a vacation? Do the children have sports or academic coaching camps already scheduled?

Parents, if there is ever a family planning session in which to practice listening, this is it. In your Summer Opportunity discussion, you have the opportunity to be a "player-coach." In a sense, you're going to mentor your child as she comes up with some of her own interests. You will also be directly involved as the one to make the introductions, provide the transportation, or hand over the funds necessary to take advantage of the opportunities.

Summer seems endless for some parents, whereas teens often wish it would never end. Working together, parents and kids can more effectively plan to enjoy the months ahead.

"I want my four children to know two things about their father. The first thing I stress with them is actually more of a mantra. At bedtime most nights I say, 'I'm going to love you forever, no matter what.' I want my children to feel loved and to know they can confide in me even in the worst of circumstances. The second and equally important

thing I want them to understand has to do with my role as a father. I have frequently needed to remind my children I'm here to be their father, not their friend. As their father, I have the responsibility of teaching them right from wrong and how to be a good citizen. Whenever the point needs to be revisited, I ask them, 'Would you rather I was your friend or your father?' Their preference is always to have a father rather than another friend."

—Marc, father of four, Los Angeles, CA

Concluding thoughts

Parenting is a journey: a journey across an ever-changing landscape of emotional peaks and valleys. Middle school presents a series of unique challenges all within the span of a few years. Physical changes coupled with a growing desire to become independent add to the frenzy of social and academic activity that kids experience on a daily basis. Parents may be left wondering how their once-tranquil child could have become the person they now see. How do parents navigate the transition from childhood to adolescence? Sadly, the majority of conversations I shared with parents in researching this book focused on a recurring theme of frustration. "Middle school is simply a matter of survival for parents and kids," one mom shared.

As we bring our journey together to a close, my hope for you is that you take action on the resources and information in this book. Scan the table of contents or flip back through the pages in search of one strategy or idea that you could likely act on in the coming week. Committing to a course in the next seven days ensures change in the short term and sets the stage for a long-term commitment to change. Sending an email to a member of your child's support team qualifies as action.

Take it slow. Parenting is a process that happens over time. My own parents still comment on the fact that although their role has changed they will always feel the responsibility and passion that comes with being a parent.

Traversing the middle school years has become a treacherous passage for families. Undoubtedly a lot has changed since your own days as a middle schooler. The internet revolution swept around the world and into homes within the span of a decade. You may not have been born in the digital age, but as a parent of a child who was, you must make it your business to learn more about the tools that affect our world.

How can parents possibly assume responsibility for tackling all of the issues facing our youth today? They can't—not if they try to do it alone. After reading this guide you have become aware of the power that comes from sharing responsibility for your child's development with a trusted group of teachers, coaches, and mentors. It takes courage to place your faith in your team to guide you through the gauntlet of questions, issues, and changes; keep in mind that this is an ongoing process. Relinquishing your position as the sole manager of your child's life to become a player on the team—albeit a key member—will tug at the very fabric of your being. Along with the discomfort you feel will come equal amounts of joy and fulfillment. Watching your child grow to become an independent person is truly an amazing experience.

Taking time to acknowledge and celebrate the small wins in your child's life builds momentum for the bigger achievements to come. Finding a new peer group that supports your child's unique personality can be every bit as fulfilling as bringing home a stellar report card. With a positive peer group, kids find the self-confidence to explore new interests, take risks, and pursue life-long passions. The importance and power of peer support cannot be overemphasized. Confronting negative social situations like cliques and bullies is likely to be an inevitable part of the middle school experience. Yet when children are surrounded by a group of supportive peers, these troubling situations can be diminished or overcome.

Standing on the sidelines while your child explores the world may be one of parenting's greatest challenges. For over a decade your child has looked to you for guidance and daily reminders of the role you play in his life. The first time you get the request to keep your distance can be quite a shock. Resist the temptation to hold onto the relationship you once had with your child. Walking hand in hand, singing lullabies, and swinging in the park are memories from a magical time. The connection you share in the coming years will be different. Different doesn't mean your child will love you less. Nevertheless, the change in connection will tug at your heart and leave you feeling alone at times. Don't despair. The short, impromptu conversations you share in the car or in the moments before your child falls asleep at night may be the glue that holds you together. Practice patience.

When your child won't talk, yet you feel sure there is something she needs to talk about, call a friend. Relying on a team of teachers, coaches, and mentors for ongoing updates can provide you with the needed insight to remain sane during times when your child becomes tight-lipped—a regular occurrence among middle schoolers. It takes time to develop relationships. Building a team starts in the months before middle school begins. Take time to appreciate the people who will share the coming years with your family.

Above all, enjoy the journey.

RECOMMENDED RESOURCES

Bullying
READING

Beane, Allan L. *The Bully Free Classroom: Over 100 Tips and Strategies for Teachers K–8*. Minneapolis, MN: Free Spirit Publishing Inc., 2005.

Romain, Trevor. *Bullies Are a Pain in the Brain*. Minneapolis, MN: Free Spirit Publishing Inc., 1997.

Romain, Trevor. *Cliques, Phonies, and Other Baloney*. Minneapolis, MN: Free Spirit Publishing Inc., 1998.

Simmons, Rachel. *Odd Girl Out: The Hidden Culture of Girls' Aggression*. Orlando, FL: Harcourt Books, 2002.

Wiseman, Rosaland. *Queen Bees and Wannabes: Helping Your Daughter Survive Cliques, Gossip, Boyfriends, and Other Realities of Adolescence*. New York, NY: Three Rivers Press, 2002.

WEBSITES

www.bullypolice.org
www.isafe.org
www.kidpower.org
www.pacerkidsagainstbullying.org

www.safeyouth.org
www.stopbullyingnow.com
www.stopcyberbullying.org

Drugs and alcohol
READING

DuPont, Robert L. *The Selfish Brain: Learning from Addiction*. Center City, MN: Hazelden, 2000.

Emmett, David, and Graeme Nice. *Understanding Street Drugs: A Handbook of Substance Misuse for Parents, Teachers, and Other Professionals.* Philadelphia, PA: Jessica Kingsley Publishers, 2006.

Falkowski, Carol. *Dangerous Drugs: An Easy-to-Use Reference for Parents and Professionals.* Center City, MN: Hazelden, 2003.

Folkers, Gladys, and Jeanne Engelmann. *Taking Charge of My Mind and Body: A Girls' Guide to Outsmarting Alcohol, Drug, Smoking, and Eating Problems.* Minneapolis, MN: Free Spirit Publishing Inc., 1997.

Godfrey, Neale S., and Rhett. *The Teen Code: How to Talk to Us about Sex, Drugs, and Everything Else—Teenagers Reveal What Works Best.* New York, NY: Rodale Books, 2004.

Kuhn, Cynthia. *Just Say Know: Talking with Kids about Drugs and Alcohol.* New York, NY: W.W. Norton & Company, Inc., 2002.

Palmiero, Karen. *90 Ways to Keep Your Kids Drug Free.* Parker, CO: Outskirts Press, Inc., 2004.

Rogers, Peter D., and Lea Goldstein. *Drugs and Your Kids: How to Tell If Your Child Has a Drug/Alcohol Problem and What to Do about It.* Oakland, CA: New Harbinger Publications, 2002.

Schwebel, Robert. *Saying No Is Not Enough—Helping Your Kids Make Wise Decisions about Alcohol, Tobacco, and Other Drugs.* New York, NY: Newmarket Press, 1998.

WEBSITES

www.freevibe.com
www.theantidrug.com

Friendship
READING

Borba, Michele. *Nobody Likes Me, Everybody Hates Me: The Top 25 Friendship Problems and How to Solve Them.* San Francisco, CA: Jossey-Bass, 2005.

General adolescence
READING

Clifford-Posten, Andrea. *Tweens: What to Expect From—and How to Survive—Your Child's Pre-Teen Years.* Oxford, England: Oneworld Publications, 2005.

Fox, Annie. *Be Confident in Who You Are (Middle School Confidential Series).* Minneapolis, MN: Free Spirit Publishing Inc., 2008.

Glasser, William. *For Parents and Teenagers: Dissolving the Barrier between You and Your Teen.* New York, NY: HarperCollins Publishers, 2002.

Godfrey, Neale S., and Rhett. *The Teen Code: How to Talk to Us about Sex, Drugs, and Everything Else—Teenagers Reveal What Works Best.* New York, NY: Rodale Books, 2004.

Goldberg, Donna. *The Organized Student: Teaching Children the Skills for Success in School and Beyond.* New York, NY: Simon & Schuster, Inc., 2005.

Grigsby, Connie, and Kent Julian. *How to Get Your Teen to Talk to You.* Sisters, OR: Multnomah Publishers, Inc., 2002.

Hartley-Brewer, E. *Talking to Tweenies.* London, England: Hodder and Stoughton, 2004.

Paterson, Kathy. *Every Adult's Guide to Talking to Teens.* Markham, Ontario: Pembroke Publishers, 2001.

Peterson, Jean Sunde. *The Essential Guide to Talking with Teens: Ready-to-Use Discussions for School and Youth Groups.* Minneapolis, MN: Free Spirit Publishing Inc., 2006.

Rainey, Barbara, and Bruce Nygren. *Parenting Today's Adolescent: Helping Your Child Avoid the Traps of the Preteen and Teen Years.* Nashville, TN: Thomas Nelson, Inc., 2002.

Rosenfeld, Alven. *The Over-Scheduled Child: Avoiding the Hyper-Parenting Trap.* New York, NY: St. Martin's Press, 2001.

Walsh, David, and Nat Bennett. *Why Do They Act That Way? A Survival Guide to the Adolescent Brain for You and Your Teen.* New York, NY: Free Press, 2005.

WEBSITES

www.helpyourteens.com

www.warningsigns.com

www.OnTeensToday.com

www.webmd.com

www.raisingkids.com

Internet safety

READING

Ensor, Jim. *Future Net: The Essential Guide to Internet and Technology Mega-trends.* Victoria, BC: Trafford Publishing, 2006.

Holloway, Sarah, and Gill Valentine. *Cyberkids: Youth Identities and Communities in an On-line World.* New York, NY: RoutledgeFalmer, 2003.

Myracle, Laruen. *TTYL (Talk To You Later).* New York, NY: Harry N. Abrams, Inc., 2005.

Young, Kimberly. *Caught in the Net: How to Recognize the Signs of Internet Addiction.* Hoboken, NJ: John Wiley & Sons, Inc., 1998.

WEBSITES

www.bewebaware.com

http://multimedia.boston.com/ pub/tn/1/featured_videos. htm?bctid=1591628237

www.cybercrime.gov

www.cybersmartcurriculum.org

www.getnetwise.org

www.netsmartz.org

www.ikeepsafe.org

www.notmykid.org

www.isafe.org

www.safekids.com

www.learnthenet.com

www.webwisekids.com

www.livewires.com

www.wiredkids.org

MySpace

READING

Clark, Chap, and Clark, Dee. *Disconnected: Parenting Teens in a MySpace World.* Grand Rapids, MI: Baker Books, 2007.

Kelsey, Candice M. *Generation MySpace: Helping Your Teen Survive Online Adolescence.* Jackson, TN: Da Capo Press, 2007.

Magid, Larry, and Anne Collier. *MySpace Unraveled: A Parent's Guide to Teen Social Networking.* Berkeley, CA: Peachpit Press, 2006.

Neal, Connie. *MySpace for Moms and Dads: A Guide to Understanding the Risks and the Rewards.* Grand Rapids, MI: Zondervan, 2007.

Rosen, Larry D. *Me, MySpace, and I: Parenting the Net Generation.* New York, NY: Palgrave Macmillan, 2007.

WEBSITES

www.komando.com/myspace/

www.myspace.com

www.myspacesafetytips.com

Sexuality
READING

Basso, Michael J. *The Underground Guide to Teenage Sexuality.* Minneapolis, MN: Fairview Press, 2003.

Godfrey, Neale S., and Rhett. *The Teen Code: How to Talk to Us about Sex, Drugs, and Everything Else—Teenagers Reveal What Works Best.* New York, NY: Rodale Books, 2004.

Schuster, Mark, and Justin Richardson. *Everything You Never Wanted Your Kids to Know about Sex (But Were Afraid They'd Ask): The Secrets to Surviving Your Child's Sexual Development.* New York, NY: Three Rivers Press, 2004.

Weill, Sabrina. *The Real Truth about Teens & Sex: From Hooking Up to Friends with Benefits—What Teens Are Thinking, Doing, and Talking About, and How to Help Them Make Smart Choices.* New York, NY: Perigree, 2005.

INDEX